PRE-WAR STANDARD CARS

Compiled by Brian Long and Tony Freeman

First published in Great Britain in 1991 by:
Academy Books Limited.
Copyright: 1991 Academy Books Limited.
Introduction: Copyright: A C L Freeman, 1991.
ISBN 1 873361 02 5.

Published and distributed by:
Academy Books Limited,
35 Pretoria Avenue,
London, E17 7DR.

Tel: 081 521 7647
Fax: 081 503 6655

Printed by:
Hillman Printers (Frome) Limited,
Frome,
Somerset.

PRE-WAR STANDARD CARS

Compiled by Brian Long and Tony Freeman

Other titles from Academy Books:

Lanchester Cars - 1895-1956
compiled by Tony Freeman, Brian Long and Chris Hood
Daimler and Lanchester - An Illustrated History
by Tony Freeman
Humber - An Illustrated History 1868-1976
by Tony Freeman
Hooper - The Master Coachbuilders
by Brian Long
How To Trace The History of Your Car
by Philip Riden
Post-War Standard Cars
compiled by Tony Freeman, Brian Long and Chris Hood
Performance Ford Cortinas
by Nik Davis
**Incident Closed - An Illustrated History of the Fire Service in
Coventry**
by Phil Consadine
Star Cars of the Ovals
by Jean Ruston

ACKNOWLEDGEMENTS

We have had a great deal of help from a number of people, including Roger Morris, the Chairman, Historian and Librarian of the Standard Motor Club, Chris Janes, the Editor of the Club's magazine, and Ian Leggitt. The publishers would very much like to thank the proprietors of *The Autocar* and *Motor* magazines for their kind permission to reproduce their copyright articles.

CONTENTS

INTRODUCTION

Born in 1871 in Kensington, London, Reginald Walter Maudslay came from a family of engineers. After attending school at Marlborough, he followed family tradition and became apprenticed to a firm of civil engineers. In 1902, he left when his employer, Sir John Wolfe Barry, provided him with the capital to form his own company. *The Standard Motor Company* was formed on 2nd March 1903 with a nominal share capital of £5,000. Of this £3,000 was contributed by Maudslay's former employer, with the remainder of the funding being provided by Alexander Gibb, Rustat Blake and Maudslay himself.

It is said that the name "Standard" arose from a conversation between Maudslay and another shareholder, Alex Craig. Craig was enthused with some of the new ideas on automotive engineering which were emerging in 1903 and it is said that his *"imagination was getting the better of his judgement"* Maudslay unimpressed, said *"I don't want any of these new ideas Mr Craig, I want my car to be composed purely of those components whoses principles have been tried and tested and accepted as reliable standards, in fact, I will name my car the Standard car."*

A small factory in Coventry's Much Park Street was taken, where the first Standard car was constructed. In January 1902, Maudslay had sketched a car which he had described as a "Motor Victoria" and by the summer of 1903 the chassis emerged from the workshop. This was a small single-cylinder machine with an underfloor engine. Later, a body was fitted and the car was used for some time in experimental form. Although fully fitted and equipped for road use it never went into production.

The second car built was a 12/15HP, costing £367, which was exhibited at the Crystal Palace Motor Show in February 1904 and later purchased by Alexander Gibb. The car was also available with four-cylinder engines as optional units. By 1904, the workforce of the Standard Motor Company had expanded to 20 men, but rapid expansion from 1905, when Standard cars were mainly sold to members and friends of the Maudslay family, to 1906 when 100 men were required to cope with increasing sales, lead to the purchase of larger premises at Bishopsgate Green, which were later to be used by Charlesworth, the coachbuilders and by Lea-Francis the motor car and cycle manufacturers. By this time, the working capital of the company had been exhausted, a situation that had arisen through the company's failure to invoice its customers for the repairs to their cars!

In 1906, Standard offered the country's first economy six-cylinder car, a relatively high powered vehicle. Powered by a side-valve engine and equipped with a three-speed gearbox and shaft drive, the range included a 24/30HP priced at £725, a 3.3 litre 20HP and a large 50HP car priced at £850.

In 1907, effective control of the Company passed to Charles Friswell, a London-based distributor. Friswell was an entrepreneur, and a seeker after Royal patronage. His London showrooms in Albany Street were renowned for their generous facilities for prospective customers. At this time the normal method of funding expansion in the motor industry was by means of an overdraft secured by the directors' personal guarantee. It is not clear why Maudslay couldn't secure the sum of £10,000 needed at this time, but the recruitment of men of substantial private means as directors of motor companies was a feature of this period, when banks were most reluctant to fund capital projects. Friswell had guaranteed Standard's borrowings at Barclays Bank and was the sole distributor of Standard cars. By 1907, Maudslay had become a salaried Director without a share in the firm's profits, with Friswell taking the position of Chairman.

Whilst six-cylinder cars were to dominate the Standard range in the years leading to the First World War, although as early as 1909 Maudslay had submitted proposals for light cars which had been shelved as a result of Friswell's preference for larger vehicles produced in small batches, much against the will of Maudslay and the rest of the Standard Board. This preference was understandable given Charles Friswell's ambitions to supply vehicles to the authorities and the Royal family.

Sailing to India in 1911, Friswell's activities resulted in the following report in *The Autocar* of 29th April 1911:

"He has succeeded in impressing the Government of India with the desirability of Standard cars under all circumstances. Sir Charles has entered into a contract with the authorities concerned to provide all the cars necessary for the proper entertainment for the guests at the Durbar Coronation ceremonies in December next. He has also made a contract with the Vice-Regal department for the provision of Standard cars for the whole of the Royal Suite, and last, but not least, Sir Charles is to provide two Standard cars for the personal use of H M King George during the Durbar celebrations. Ten Standard lorries will be supplied for the carriage of beaters in connection with the tiger hunting

R W Maudslay

expeditions which will, of course, form part of the Royal programme, and two more for the transportation of the general impedimenta. Adequately to carry out these undertakings Sir Charles contemplates the despatch of no less than 100 Standard cars to India for this purpose."

In fact, 70 cars were despatched to India, including a six-cylinder Landaulette with Royal blue coachwork for the use of the King.

Having provided an overdraft of £10,000 which had enabled the Company to obtain premises in Coventry, Friswell's own distributorship failed to meet their financial obligations to Standard in 1912, enabling Maudslay to free himself of Friswell's influence with the assitance of C J Band, a well-known Coventry solicitor who was subsequently Chairman of the Company, and Seigfried Bettman, founder of the Triumph Cycle Company, who had taken over the chair in 1911.

Meanwhile, Standard continued to develop it's range of cars with the introduction of the 2.7 litre four-cylinder model in 1909. Four-cylinder cars gradually replaced the ageing six-cylinder models, which were phased out in 1912. In 1913, the 9.5HP Standard Light Car, priced at £185, was announced. This featured a three-speed gearbox and worm drive, and all braking was applied to the rear wheels! Electric lighting was made available and was later fitted to the 2.4 litre and 3.3 litre cars introduced on the eve of the First World War. In May 1914, a model "S" 9.5HP light car was entered in the RAC Light Car Trial, where it was among only 8 cars finishing from the 32 starters and gained a gold medal for its performance.

The 9.5HP was subsequently offered with a selection of body styles and production continued until May 1915. The model was a modest success and represented the firm's first serious attempt at mass-production, with 1,933 being made before car production was suspended in 1915.

With the coming of the First World War, Standard cars failed to attract government interest, so the factory was initially contracted to produce munitions. Shells and trench mortars were the main output in 1914-1915, although the company was later awarded the contract to produce RE8 bi-planes in 1915, thereafter being brought under government supervision as a "controlled establishment". During the war, the company produced some 1,600 aircraft, the best-known being the Sopwith Pup.

Orders were first placed in May 1916, with output reaching 24 aeroplanes per week which were supplied to the Royal Air Force, The Royal Australian Air Force and the Japanese Government. Unfortunately, the first Standard-produced Pup had the unenviable distinction of being captured behind enemy lines near Bapaume on 4th January 1917. Although Standard shared in the design and manufacture of other aircraft and components during the war, Maudslay's preference was for

A delightful 1931 Standard 16hp Avon Coupe.

the manufacture of motor vehicles. In March 1917, Standard's directors applied for government authority to commence experimental work on cars in order to "*enable the Company to be in a position to resume their ordinary trade after hostilities have ceased.*"

By July 1917, applications for patents relating to improvements to carburettors and electrical fittings were lodged and Maudslay later announced to shareholders that a new vehicle would shortly be available. This, together with other technical developments, placed the Company in a strong position to resume car production at the cessation of hostilities in 1918.

Of much greater long term importance was the acquisition of premises which enabled the Company to later become a mass-producer of cars. A former skating rink in Leamington Spa was purchased in 1916 and additional rented accommodation was found in the town. The most significant acquisition, however, was the purchase of a 30-acre site from Lord Leigh in 1915. Initially intended for aircraft construction, the buildings on the site were extended and a subsequent purchase of a further 110 acres adjacent to the main Canley works which later became the main centre of Standard's operations. These significant investments were paid for from profits accruing from government contracts, some of which made provision for advance payment for both aircraft and the facilities needed to manufacture them. This, together with a series of bank loans underwritten by debenture issues, placed Standard in an enviable position amongst Britain's car manufacturers at the end of the war.

However, some difficulty was experienced in 1918, particularly with liquidity, largely because of the late payment on some war-time government contracts which resulted in a £130,000 overdraft. This impeded the production and development of new vehicles and only 350 vehicles were manufactured in 1919. Completion of government orders further delayed the return to car manufacture and the Company resorted to the re-introduction of pre-war models. It was not until 1921 that a new Standard model was introduced, the "SLO" tourer. A four seater family car, it sold well, not least because it featured an effective weather-proof hood and side screens designed by Maudslay himself. An OHV 8HP model was introduced for the 1922 season followed by a 13.9HP SLO4 in 1924, priced at £375. By this time Standard radiators were carrying the emblem of the Ninth Roman Legion and 10,000 of the cars were sold during 1924, putting the firm's output on a par with Austin.

In 1926 front-wheel brakes were introduced on the 13.9 HP cars and the following year a 2.2 litre o.h.v. six-cylinder model was introduced, but this did not prove to be much of a success. In 1927, Alfred Wilde, from Morris Engines in Coventry was appointed Chief Engineer. Wasting little time, by 1928 his efforts resulted in the introduction of the 1195cc Standard "Nine", with side-valve engine and fabric coachwork. This was not an immediate success, requiring restyling and re-launching, but further cars based on the Standard Nine chassis followed. These included a longer wheelbase model, a sports two-seater and the first of a series of specials with bodies by Avon Coachworks, a low slung two-seater designed by the Jensen brothers. These Avons, both in this form and utilising other Standard chassis, would stay in production for the next decade.

In 1929, a series of side-valve sixes was introduced with coil ignition and seven-bearing crankshafts. This new line was to continue until 1940, when following the outbreak of war, passenger car production was virtually suspended until 1946. By 1931 a small saloon, the Big Nine, which was priced at under £200, had been introduced, together with low-priced sixes rated at 16 and 20HP respectively.

The Nines soon gained a reputation for reliaility, much of this resulting from Wilde's

Standard cars were successful in competitive events, as this 1933 model on the 1934 Welsh Trial demonstrates.

innovations. An example was his practice of displaying prototype parts as soon as they were available from the experimental shops, so that the production engineers could examine them and suggest any design changes before the parts were sent for manufacture. A second example was the introduction of prototype and production vehicle testing day and night between Coventry and North Wales. However, no Board appointment was forthcoming and in 1930 Wilde accepted an offer to join Rootes, but fell ill and died in December 1931, aged forty-one.

Although Standard accounted for some 5% of total car production in 1929, it failed to yield it's shareholders a dividend for the five years to 1931. Part of this was because of the policy of re-investment of profit into buildings and machinery which had doubled Canley's floor space to ten acres in 1924, but also because of losses sustained with the less than successful six-cylinder car, which failed to make much impact on the contracting big-car market.

Standard was undoubtedly successful with its range of small to medium sized cars in the 1920s, although the "Nine" had had to be re-launched, following disappointing sales of the early version. Another factor which contributed to this malaise was overcommitment to a large Australian order which was withdrawn in 1927, resulting in a 25% drop in turnover compared with the previous year. This ambitious expansion into overseas markets was badly misjudged since it absorbed substantial amounts of working capital on a contract which yielded very low profit margins. By 1929, losses of £123,698 had accumulated and only the timely assistance of Barclays Bank, who allowed the Company's overdraft to stand at £160,000 into 1930, no doubt prompted by William Morris' threat to withdraw his own substantial deposits. This enabled Standard to remain independent into the 1930s, when they would have otherwise been a prime target for the Rootes brothers. Sales, market share and profits began to improve, although this was to be largely thanks to the recruitment of John Black.

In the meantime, the one-litre Little Nine was utilised by William Lyons as a basis for his SS2 car. Lyons' 1930 Swallow-bodied Standards had been up-market small saloons, still recognisable as Standards, but the SS2 used a specially commissioned Standard chassis and Lyons' own style of bodywork. Standard engines featured in all of the Lyons cars until 1940 and powered the four-cylinder Jaguars until 1948, though by this time Jaguar owned the tooling and assembled the engines themselves.

By September 1933, when record sales of 2,400 cars were reported, market share had increased to 9%, where it remained for the rest of the 1930s. Learning the lessons from the abortive Australian contract, much of this was sustained by foreign sales, where the Company traded in 33 countries and enjoyed an extensive network of dealers providing sales, spares and servicing.

At home, the domestic success of the Standard "Nine" was responsible for the firm's recovery, some 9,000 examples being manufactured in 1929-1930. By the end of 1931, Standard's share of output amongst the UK's "big six" had doubled, the Company now being a mass producer in the same league as Austin, Morris, Rootes and Ford.

Following the rise of fascist dictatorships in Europe in the 1920s and 1930s, Stanley Baldwin's

This Flying Standard "Ten" dates from around 1938, and offered comfortable and economical motoring for four.

government had concentrated on the prospect of war and in particular on the need to adapt the country's industrial base to wartime production in the event of prolonged hostilities. By February 1936, the cabinet has resolved to enter into a programme of development for the Royal Air Force which would involve the manufacture of some 8,000 new fighter and bomber aircraft. Both government and industry perceived the need for additional facilities if these ambitious plans were ever to be realised.

A meeting was convened for May 1936, to be chaired by the Secretary of State for Air, and its participants included John Black of Standard, Sir Geoffrey Burton of Daimler, Spencer Wilks of Rover and Lord Austin. The result of these discussions was the commencement of the Shadow Factory schemes and the building of Standard's first Shadow Factory at Canley, and Standard's second at Banner Lane, the largest in the scheme, being a 1 million square-foot complex.

Inclusion of Standard in the Shadow Factory scheme was public recognition of Standard's recovery from near bankruptcy in the late 1920s. This success was attributed to the 9HP models of the 1930s and the 1.3 litre 10HP of 1934, which proved to be a best seller. In 1936 the first of the Flying Standards had been introduced, which featured the distinctive fastback look and the novel boot. The 12HP Flying Standard was followed by a 16HP and the top-of-the-range 20HP, featuring a six-cylinder 2663cc side-valve engine and priced at £315. In 1937, the introduction of the two-door 8HP at £129 featured independent front suspension, the first time this feature had been offered on a British small car. This car was also a best seller, and deservedly so. Less successful was the 2.7 litre V8 of the same year, although the engine was subsequently used to power five of the Raymond Mays sports cars of 1938/39.

In a small way the Standard car also enjoyed an enduring popularity with the Royal family, particularly the Duke of Gloucester, who took delivery of a 16HP Saloon in 1933 and presented a Flying Twenty to the Duchess in 1936. The first car owned by the Duke of Edinburgh was a Standard Flying Nine in 1939.

Much of the credit for the change in the Company's fortunes must go to John Black. Born in 1895 in Kingston, Surrey, Black studied law and is believed to have been involved with a firm dealing with patents for Morgan prior to his seeing active service during the First World War.

Following demobilisation in 1919, he joined Hillman and later married one of Hillman's six daughters. In 1929 he moved to Standard where he was initially Maudslay's personal assistant. Appointed General Manager in 1929, Black became Standard's joint Managing Director in 1931 with Reginald Maudslay and following Maudslay's death in 1934, he became the sole occupant of that office.

Black's main strength was in his organisational skills which applied common-sense and military precision to the re-organisation of virtually all aspects of the Standard operation from the production line to the work's outing. By 1931, the whole of the assembly shops had been re-organised and mechanised to facilitate mass production, with ten complete cars leaving the line every hour. By October 1932, sales had increased 80% on the previous year and profits had almost trebled. This emphasis on the organisation of production was to result in output increasing from 8,000 vehicles in 1931 to 34,000 in 1936, 40,000 in 1937 and 55,000 in 1939, without any significant increase in the workforce.

Part of this recovery resulted from the introduction of a system of bonus payments on a team output basis which was designed to stimulate greater personal effort and productivity amongst the workforce. Overall labour relations were reasonably healthy, reflecting a benevolent paternalism and the firm's improving financial status. An example of this approach was the introduction of paid holidays in 1937, expressed by the directors as "something in the way of distribution as part of the profits to the work people was required."

Remarking on John Black's contribution in 1938, Standard's chairman said:

"*To his enthusiasm, his untiring energy, his far sighted grasp of the motor industry and his loyalty to the company....I attribute very largely the position in which the company stands today, not only in the motor industry but in the country as a whole.*"

However, Black dominated the Board of the Company for 20 years in a way which was ultimately destructive. His management style was notoriously dictatorial, and those who did not resign lived in fear of Black, who cultivated his fearsome reputation with his executives, whilst relaxing discipline with the workforce. One visitor to Standard was alarmed to find when conveyed to Black's office that: "*the large de-luxe office was, I imagine, similar to Mussolinni's in its heyday.*"

The unnecessary authoritarian style with his management ultimately resulted in Black's own Board, headed by Alick Dick, ousting him on New Year's day, 1954. The lack of a consistent, disciplined approach to labour relations ultimately resulted in post-war productivity declining to the point where Standard-Triumph became an easy take-over target for the ambitious Leyland Group. Had Standard been able to address the crucial problems of succession and management style before this, it may have been possible for strong management to have changed the company's direction in this important period of its development.

The last Standard was produced in 1963 and the marque has since begun to fade from the public domain. However, it was one of the most popular British cars prior to the Second World War providing unpretentious and economic motoring for many satisfied customers. Despite the enormous pre-war output of the company, relatively few examples of the cars survive compared with the remainder of the "big-six" motor manufacturers. Of those that do remain, many fine examples of the cars are preserved by the membership of the Standard Motor Club and a smaller number are preserved in Museum collections throughout the UK.

This book traces the development of the Standard car as seen by the contemporary motoring journals, and contains road tests, technical data and previously unpublished photographs of a number of cars. A companion volume, *Post-War Standard Cars,* deals with the immediate post-war range of Standard cars until the marque's demise in 1963.

Tony Freeman
March 1991

THE STANDARD CAR.

SINGLE OR DOUBLE CYLINDER—5in. BORE, 3in. STROKE, SPEED 250 TO 2000 R.P.M. —SLIDING TYPE CHANGE SPEED GEAR, THREE SPEEDS AND REVERSE – BEVEL GEAR TRANSMISSION ON TO LIVE AXLE – A NEW GIRDER FRAME.

A car which seems destined to make its mark is now being built by the Standard Motor Co., of Coventry. There are several novel features in the design and construction of the vehicle, and these should be carefully noted by those who peruse the following description of its mechanism, as some are distinctly striking.

The Framework, Springs, and Axles.

The side members of the frame are constructed of H section rolled steel. The forward end has a long V-shaped piece removed, and the ends are then closed together, and electrically welded at the place where the metal is removed so as to form the tapered forward end of the side members. The rear ends are similarly treated, though they remain straight as to the upper edge of the girder, the lower edge being tapered upward, giving the side member the form usually assumed by a pressed steel frame. The side members are joined together by seven transverse members of channel section. Two of these plates at about the centre of the car support the gear box, and the two forward ones support the engine. The forward member, as well as holding together the side plates, also supports the radiator. Brackets carrying the front and rear springs are bolted to the ends of the side and rear cross members. The frame is supported on elliptical springs, 3ft. in length, both fore and aft. The front attachment of the spring is made in sections, being drilled out to receive the anchored end of the forward spring. These sections are bolted together to the central web of the frame, the ends of the bolts being afterwards riveted over, so as to preclude all possibility of their working loose. The same bolt which serves to anchor the forward end of the spring also holds together the two sections of the

front spring iron. The springs are provided with exceptionally long links so as to give them plenty of free motion. The forward axle consists of tube 1⅝in. in diameter and 1in. bore. In this instance the stud axles are provided with arms embracing the fixed axle ends. Additional support is given to the forward end of the frame by means of a rod which is used to carry the headlight. Brackets are provided on the frame at one end to form a hinge for the lamp-bracket rod, and at the other for a key bolt, which bolt is always kept in engagement by means of a helical spring. When it is necessary to start the engine, instead of the lamp having to be removed the key bolt is lifted, and the whole of the lamp bracket swung back.

The Engine.

There are two types of car, one having a single cylinder engine, and the other a two-cylinder engine. The single cylinder engine is of 8 h.p. This has a bore of 5in. and stroke 3in. The normal power is developed at 1,200 revolutions per minute. This speed may be accelerated up to as high as 2,000 revolutions per minute, and the engine will continue to run at as slow a speed as 250. The valves are placed side by side, and both are mechanically operated. The forward end of the camshaft is enclosed, and directly attached thereto is the water circulating pump, on the end of the spindle of which is carried the commutator. The connection between the pump and the commutator spindle and the camshaft proper is made by means of a positive jaw coupling. The governor is mounted on the forward end of the crankshaft, and is of the usual centrifugal ball type, engaging in collar with a sliding sleeve. The governor has a fork connected to the throttle valve in the carburetter by suitable connections.

One of the earliest complete Standard cars. Larger wheels and an improved body are now used.

Carburetter and Regulating Mechanism.

The action of the carburetter and combined throttle is shown in fig. 2. The petrol enters at A into the float chamber B in the usual manner, and passes thence to the nipple C, communication with which

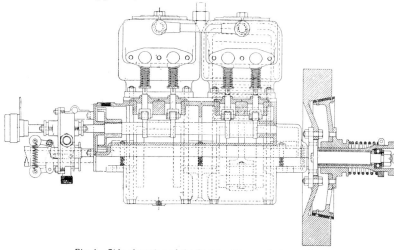

Fig. 1.—Side elevation of the Standard two-cylinder engine.

is effected along the port D, past a belt mouthed cone through the body E, and through the valves F and G, which can be rotated by the levers H and I respectively. The gas passes through slots in the two valves G and H, and is carried by passages along to the inlet valves. The whole casting is bolted up quite close to the cylinders, by means of four bolts. The valve F acts not only as a throttle but also as an air regulator. The governor sleeve lever is attached to H, and when the governor opens, the slot J in valve G is moved over by the slot K in valve F. The result is that, although there is a movement on the valve F from the governor, no difference is made in the orifice in the valve G until the edge of the slot K comes over to the remote edge of the slot J, after which the valve H commences to cut off the supply of gas to the engine, and totally cuts off when the fore edge of slot K comes up to the inner edge of slot J. Before this valve commences to cut off, however, the slot L in valve F begins to move over the slot M in the body of the casting E, with the result that an increased opening for an additional supply of air is given. When the engine is at rest this opening is closed, and it attains its maximum opening when the engine is running at its maximum speed. The shape of this opening, as will be seen, follows a curve which has been carefully gone into, and gives correct mixture at every range of engine speed. To cut out the action of the governor valve G may be operated by the lever I, by means of a hand lever mounted on the steering wheel, and can be so worked as to follow the slot in valve F, and thus not allow the cut off to take place. This hand throttle G can be set so that the engine can be made to cut out at any speed from 250 up to 2,000 revolutions per minute, by a simple movement of a hand lever on the steering wheel. The simplicity of this method of governing can be readily seen, and in practice gives perfect results.

The Two-cylinder Engine.

The two-cylinder engine has precisely similar dimensions to the single cylinder engine, the con-

structional features being two independent single cylinders attached to an enlarged crankcase. The cranks are set at 180 degrees, running in three phosphor bronze bearings, the central one being purposely stiff. Lubrication of the piston is by sight feed lubricators, and that of the connecting rod ends and crankshaft bearings by splash. While on the subject of splash lubricating, it is interesting to note that this may sometimes be carried out to an abnormal extent without any fear of fouling the sparking plug. If this is placed immediately over the inlet valve it is always surrounded by the richest portion of the mixture, while the exhaust gases subject it to a slight scouring action, which contributes to its cleanly qualities. There is a circulating pump of the rotary gear type, delivering water to the bottom of the cylinders, the water circulating completely round the cylinders and valve chambers, and passing thence to the top of the honeycomb radiator, behind which is placed an open fan, belt-driven, which creates an abnormally strong draught, thus ensuring efficient cooling.

Fig. 2.—The Standard carburetter and governor.

A, petrol intake
B, float feed chamber
C, spraying nipple
D, air intake
E, carburetter and governor body
F, governor throttle valve and air regulator
G, hand throttle valve
H, lever operating F
I, lever operating G
J slot in G
K,, slot in F
L, air regulating slot
M, extra air inlet

(To be continued.)

THE STANDARD CAR.

SINGLE OR DOUBLE CYLINDER—5in. BORE, 3in. STROKE, SPEED 250 TO 2000 R.P.M.
—SLIDING TYPE CHANGE SPEED GEAR, FOUR SPEEDS AND REVERSE–BEVEL GEAR
TRANSMISSION ON TO LIVE AXLE–A NEW GIRDER FRAME.

(Continued from page 725.)

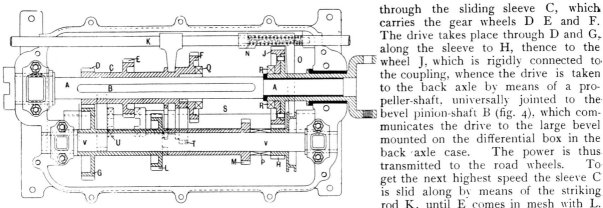

Fig. 3.—Plan of change speed gear.

A A, primary gearshaft	J, gear wheel on A A carrying propeller connection.	P, jaw clutch
B, feather on A A	K, rod carrying gear changing fork.	Q and R, jaw clutches.
C, sliding sleeve on A A.		S, reverse gearshaft.
D, slow speed pinion.	L, second speed gear wheel.	T, sliding sleeve for reverse gear.
E, second speed gear wheel.	M, third speed gear wheel.	U, reverse gear jaw clutch.
F, third speed gear wheel.	N, boss on the rod K.	V V, secondary gearshaft.
G slow speed gear wheel	O, tongue piece operating high speed gear.	
H, pinion on secondary shaft V V.		

The Change-speed Gear.

The change-speed gear is of the sliding tooth variety, and gives four speeds forward and one reverse. In the low speed the drive is taken through a coupling from the engineshaft to the shaft A (fig. 3), through long keys, two in number, B ; thence through the sliding sleeve C, which carries the gear wheels D E and F. The drive takes place through D and G, along the sleeve to H, thence to the wheel J, which is rigidly connected to the coupling, whence the drive is taken to the back axle by means of a propeller-shaft, universally jointed to the bevel pinion-shaft B (fig. 4), which communicates the drive to the large bevel mounted on the differential box in the back axle case. The power is thus transmitted to the road wheels. To get the next highest speed the sleeve C is slid along by means of the striking rod K, until E comes in mesh with L. The power is then taken from E to L and along the sleeve to H and J, thence through the propeller-shaft. For the third highest speed the sleeve C is slid further along until F comes into mesh with M, the drive being thus taken along to H and J as before. For the top speed the sleeve is slid still further, until the striking rod K, which carries a boss, comes in contact with the boss N. This moves a tongue piece O, engaging with a boss on the pinion H, until H is brought out of mesh with J, although it is still

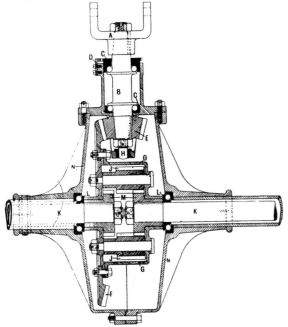

Fig. 4.—Section of bevel gear drive and differential.

A, propeller-shaft connection	H, end bearing to B
B, bevel pinion shaft	J J, star pinions to differential gear
C C, ball bearings to B	
D, adjustment for C C	K K, divided live axle
E, bevel pinion	L L, ball bearings on K K
F, bevel gear wheel	M, star wheels on K K
G G, differential gear box	N N, gear box

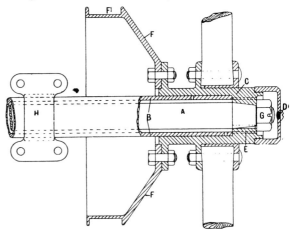

Fig. 5.—Section of rear hub bearing.

A, end of live axle	F F, band brake drum
B, tube enclosing A	F¹, groove for band brake
C, wheel hub	G, lock nut to axle A
D, hub cap oil screw	H, spring plate
E, oil ways	

engaged by the jaw clutches P, with the sleeve carrying N. Thus, all wheels are thrown out of mesh, and any further movement of the rod K brings the jaws Q into mesh with the jaws R, and thus the shaft A is really made solid with the gear J, and a direct drive with all wheels out of mesh is the result, thus getting a most efficient through drive. To obtain the reverse, a third or auxiliary shaft S, mounted on bearings below the two mainshafts, carries a sliding sleeve T, which has square jaw faces at one end and a pinion on the other, which pinion is brought into mesh with L, when the striking rod K moves this to the left. Of course, in the meantime the striking rod K has moved the gear pinion D out of mesh with G, and any further movement of the sleeve T brings the square jaw clutch on T into contact with the square jaw clutch

Fig. 6.—The two-cylinder Standard engine in position. This shows the accessibility of the motor and its relative height.

at U, thus meshing. At the same time the gear wheel E is brought into mesh with the gear wheel rigidly connected with U. Thus the reverse is obtained in a somewhat similar manner to that employed by the idle gear wheel when engaged in cutting a screw on the lathe. When reducing the gear from the top speed to the third, the jaws Q and R are first released from contact, and under the action of a spring shown at N, the pinion H is again restored into gear with the wheel J, and thus all is ready for the forward drive on the next lower speed. The gear case top is simply a cover having an inspection lid, so that the gear may be viewed without removing this cover, or oil and grease may be placed in the case in large quantities. The bearings are adjustable without interfering with the facing of the case, so that an oil or greasetight joint is always kept, this being an important factor in preserving the bearings when adjustment is required.

In the back axle hub bearing the bending stress is entirely removed from the driving shaft A (fig 5), and a bearing is formed on the outer diameter of the tubular axle B. The body of the back hub C is made of good bearing metal—phosphor bronze—and a long bearing is thus secured, which takes the weight direct from the road wheels. Lubrication is effected both by the grease working along from the bevel gear box in the centre of the axle, and also by oiling through the cap D, whence the lubricant works its way through the oil holes E. Thus very little attention is required in this direction. The brake drum F is mounted concentric with the hub, and is tightly held by bolts, as shown. The spring flaps are brought closely up to this brake drum, and support the brake brackets in a very strong and

rigid manner, so that absolutely no spring can take place in the application of the brakes, so very great braking power is exerted. The driving-shaft A is secured to the hub C by means of a tapered part, also by wide keys, and a lock nut G as shown.

The Live Axle.

The rear end of the propeller-shaft is attached to the coupling A (fig. 4), secured to the pinion-shaft B, which rotates in an easily adjustable ball bearing C C. This bearing very closely resembles that used in the ordinary bicycle, the details of which are sufficiently well known to make this piece of mechanism perfectly simple of being understood. The adjustment of the bearing is effected by an outside cap, which is secured in position by means of a catch D. On the inner end of B is carried a bevel pinion E, and this engages with the bevel gear wheel F, secured to the differential gear box G G. The inner extremity of the bevel pinion-shaft B, it will be seen, is supported by a plain bearing H. This is one of the very few instances in which the end of the bevel pinion-shaft is so supported, and it is very obvious that this must conduce to very steady running, as it equalises the amount of thrust exerted between the bevel pinion and its gear wheel. The differential gear box G G contains a star pattern gear, the pinions of which are shown by J J, so that this type dispenses entirely with the use of bevel wheels in connection with the differential gear. The two-piece live axle K K runs as to its inner ends on ball bearings, shown by L L. They carry on their extremities the star pinions M, which engage with the differential pinions J J. The whole of this gear is enclosed in a rigid castiron box N.

The silent running of the engine is largely contributed to by the dimensions of the silencer, which are 3ft. 6in. by 7in. Though large, the silencer is not at all obtrusive.

The Control.

The carburetter is fed by gravity, the petrol tank being located beneath the front seats.

Fig. 7.—The Standard single cylinder governed engine.

A foot-brake operates expanding segments operating upon a drum directly attached to the hub. The side brakes operate bands acting upon the same drums.

All the speeds are actuated by one lever. There are four speeds forward and one reverse. The top speed equals twenty-three and a half miles per hour with the engine running at normal speed. The road wheels are 32in. in diameter. The change-speed lever is locked by means of a square segment definitely engaging with slots cut in the sector.

It has already been stated that the speed of the engine is controlled by means of the throttle lever, which is most conveniently placed on the top of the steering wheel, the actuating mechanism running through the centre of the steering column. With a little practice and observation this lever can be placed in such a position that one can be certain as to the speed of the car when travelling on the level, and this speed may be maintained by opening or closing the throttle as required. Owing to the great flexibility of the engine and the gear ratios fully seventy-five per cent. of the running may be done on the top gear; runs of great length have been accomplished without changing gear. Although four speeds are provided, the first is very seldom used, as the speed given is very slow indeed, and, unless starting on very steep hills, the second speed is used. It is very comforting, however, to know that the car has a gear which will enable it to surmount any hill, however steep, without having to shed its passengers.

Mr. A. Craig, consulting engineer, of Coventry, is responsible for the design of the Standard car, which cannot be said to contain any features of Mr. Craig's previous designs. As showing the diversity of this gentleman's work, we may mention that the Maudslay petrol locomotive, illustrations of which were given in *The Autocar* of November 14th, page 597, was designed by him.

A DOUBLE LANDAU.

The completed chassis ready to take its body.

Sketch of the completed vehicle.

combination is given so that the car can do the great majority of its work on the direct third, and at the same time have a reserve of speed when it is used for country work. The line drawing shows it as it will be when it is completed with a Windover body. The larger illustration shows the chassis complete, and the other one how access is gained to the engine, which is almost as easily get-at-able as when placed under a bonnet, though it will be noted that in this carriage the driver sits directly above his motor.

Usually in vehicles designed in this manner accessibility is not well considered, but the design we illustrate shows that every attention has been given to this point.

The illustrations we give are interesting, because they show the comparatively small alteration which is required to render the chassis of an ordinary touring car suitable for a town carriage. The chassis is that of an ordinary Standard car of 16-20 h.p., and the mechanism to all intents and purposes the same as that of the car which performed so well in the Tourist Trophy Race last year. The parts themselves are all of the standard pattern, and merely rearranged to meet the case, the only alterations being the steering connections and the radiator and special petrol and water tanks. The gear ratio on the direct third speed is four to one, the indirect drive being on the fourth speed. This slightly lower gear direct drive

View showing the arrangements made to give access to the engine.

THE 15 H.P. SIX-CYLINDER STANDARD CAR.

One rather expects a 15 h.p. six-cylinder car to be a sort of motor microism, and the preliminary announcements about the small six-cylinder Standard in the autumn rather led one to anticipate a very small car with a very small engine. In fact, this was the original idea, but the interest taken in the proposed baby six-cylinder was very great, and, strangely enough, the desire that it should be made somewhat larger was still greater, so that the original little car with a 70 mm. × 82 mm. engine and a 7ft. 3in. wheelbase has been developed into something very much larger, though we believe that the engine is still the smallest six-cylinder engine on the market to-day.

The general appearance of the chassis is plainly shown in the illustration. It will be seen that the frame is of the stamped steel variety turned up at the back to give a combination of sufficient axle clearance with low side entrance. The wheelbase is 9ft. 8in., and the track 4ft. 6in. Full elliptical springs carry the back part of the car, and the springs are connected to the main frame by strong brackets. The design throughout is about as simple as it is possible to make a car.

To turn to the engine, the six cylinders are cast in pairs, with a bore of 3½in. and a stroke of 3½in.; that is, the engine is 88 mm. × 88 mm. The valves are all on the left side. On the right-hand side is the steering box, the magneto and the pump, all up on a table at the side of the engine, and remarkably easy to get at. On the opposite side is the carburetter. As the engine is low in proportion to its length, a good high radiator can be fitted without exceeding the usual over-all dimensions. This enables sufficient natural cooling to be provided that the pump is hardly necessary, and we understand that the test cars have been run without a fan quite satisfactorily,

though a fan is always provided so as to be on the safe side. The clutch is of the single metal disc pattern. It runs in oil, and is self-contained in the flywheel.

The change-speed gear provides three speeds, with direct drive on the top. The gear cover is not a mere small lid which enables one to look into the box and see some of the gears; it is as large as the box itself,

The engine of the six-cylinder 15 h.p. Standard car. This gives a good idea of the accessibility of the steering-box, magneto, and pump. On the other side the carburetter and valves are equally get-at-able.

and when removed the whole of the gear wheels are visible. The back axle is extremely well designed, and, as is usual with Standard practice, it is easy to examine the bevel gear at any time. Both shafts in the gear box, the bevel shaft, back axle, and front wheels all run upon Hoffmann ball bearings. The back axle is a genuine ball bearing axle, in the sense that the driving shafts are entirely free from contact with the outer sleeve or weight-carrying portion of the axle. The front axle is of the

The chassis of the new 15 h.p. six-cylinder Standard car.

forged type, and on the lines of that which has proved so satisfactory for the 30 h.p. six-cylinder Standard. In fact, the 15 h.p. may be said, broadly, to be a reduced *facsimile* of the 30 h.p., though its vital parts are not shorn of any of their strength.

As one follows the design out carefully, one cannot help being struck by its extreme simplicity, and we are looking forward with interest to a trial of this new six-cylinder car. The vehicle we inspected was at the Standard factory at Coventry, but we understand that Messrs. Friswell, who are the selling agents of the Standard cars, now have it in their possession. We should, perhaps, add that no ridiculous claims are made for this car; it is not suggested that it is as good as, say, the 30 h.p. six-cylinder Standard. The idea of its introduction is to meet two wants. One is for a very sweet running and comparatively cheap town carriage with a landaulet body, and the other is to provide a simple car which will, with a slightly higher gear and a suitable open body, possess a very good turn of speed—a vehicle, in short, which can be driven almost anywhere upon its top gear.

A rather elegant Standard Tourer dating from 1909.

At a meeting of the Marine Committee of the Society of Motor Manufacturers and Traders on March 18th it was resolved to call a special meeting of the committee to consider the question of future motor boat exhibitions, and to invite the exhibitors at the recent Olympia Exhibition who are members of the Society to attend.

* * *

The details of a competition for the best design for a Motor Union almanack are published in the current number of the *Studio*. Two prizes of eight guineas and four guineas respectively are offered by the Motor Union for the best design. The almanack is not to exceed 24in. by 17½in. in size, and must be designed for printing in not more than three colours. It must give prominence to the title and address of the Motor Union, and include a design for a monthly tear-off calendar for setting forth the principal automobile events of that month. The space to be reserved for this calendar must be not less than one-fourth of the almanack. Space must also be left for a miniature calendar of the whole year. Drawings, packed flat, should reach the London office of the *Studio*, 44, Leicester Square, London, W., by May 2nd.

THE STANDARD 20 H.P. SIX-CYLINDER CAR.

This attractive and dainty chassis was only briefly touched upon in our Show review last week for the reason that it was not staged very early. It is so much one of the specialities of the Show that, given now the opportunity, we hasten to describe it in detail, and to draw attention to a few of its particular features by the aid of a few sketches. It is the first of the light six-cylinder cars, and as such deserves special attention.

The frame is of pressed channel section cambered steel slightly inswept at the dashboard and upswept at the rear of the body. It is stiffened by cross members of like section fore and aft, and centrally by a tubular member carried in flanged steel sockets riveted to the side members. Between the forward

tioned. A neat form of detachable driver connects the pump spindle and the armature spindle of the magneto. Valve caps cover the several valve chambers, and carry the sparking plugs and very neat dust-covered compression taps, the former, of course, over the induction and the latter over the exhaust valves. The exhaust is discharged through straight arms into a horizontal cast-iron exhaust pot running the entire length of the top of the cylinders, whence it proceeds through a long exhaust pipe to a short silencer, and escapes thence into the air through another length of tube, which terminates in a flattened nozzle, entirely silencing the engine. Provision is made on the right-hand side of the cylinders for the insertion of sparking plugs for use with the independent

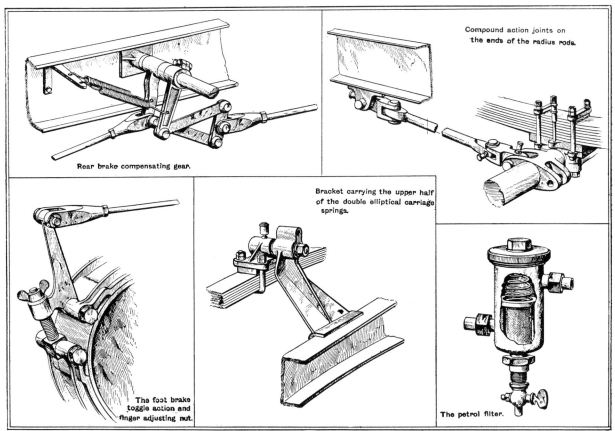

Rear brake compensating gear.

Compound action joints on the ends of the radius rods.

Bracket carrying the upper half of the double elliptical carriage springs.

The foot brake toggle action and finger adjusting nut.

The petrol filter.

Some mechanical details of the 20 h.p. six-cylinder Standard car.

member and the tubular member runs a channel section underframe supporting the engine. The rear ends of the underframe are carried in steel slings from the cross tube.

The radiator, which is, of course, of the now well-known and distinctive Standard pattern, is formed of lined flanged vertical tubing. The cylinders are cast in pairs, all valve chambers on the left-hand side, with ample water-jacket spacings round the combustion head and valve chambers. The water spacing is enclosed by oval-formed brass covers, which can be readily detached for cleaning and scaling. The distribution gear wheels are of fibre and gun-metal, and are encased. A table is formed on the right-hand side of the crank chamber, upon which the pump and magneto are most conveniently and accessibly posi-

accumulator fed ignition system if required, and a projection of the camshaft rearwards serves for bevel or worm gear attachment for the contact-maker and distributer.

The cylinder dimensions are $3\frac{1}{2}$in. stroke and $3\frac{1}{2}$in. bore, or 89 mm. by 89 mm. It may be here said that the flywheel has plenty of weight in its rim, thus further contributing to the motor's steady running.

The water circulation is exceedingly well disposed, the water continually travelling upwards from the pump until it passes through the water-jackets and out of the cylinders above the combustion chambers into the sharply raked lead to the top of the radiator. Oiling apertures enclosed by thumbscrew gun-metal covers are formed in the three left-hand brackets of the crank chamber.

The carburetter is of special design, the arrangement of which can be readily grasped by a glance at the accompanying sketch. Nothing much simpler in the form of accessibility has been done with regard to jet access. The throtle is formed of a cylindrical body of gun-metal, through which holes are bored vertically and horizontally, the first for the jet and the second for the mixture passage, and can be lifted straight out of the cylindrical casing in which it is carried, and the jet immediately exposed.

The engine is lubricated by gravity from a brass cylindrical lubricating tank set inside the bonnet on the face of the dashboard, and serving through four drip feeds on the rear of the latter. In this position the oil is always kept in a good fluid condition.

The drive passes from the engine

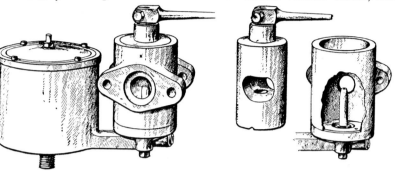

The Standard carburetter complete, and also with the throttle piston block withdrawn to expose jet.

through a well-designed form of single plate clutch, which is so mounted that it requires a very slight pressure upon the clutch pedal for its withdrawal. This clutch is enclosed, and runs in oil. The cover is very easily dismounted, and the clutch capable of being withdrawn without interference with any other unit.

A neat form of flexible joint connects the clutch-shaft to the primary gearshaft, in its very short, stiff, staunchly-carried gear box with its three-speed gear change. The gearshafts run on ball bearings. The change-speed lever operates through a compact form of gate, and the striking arms and striking lever, while being thoroughly protected from dust and mud by an apron, are placed in an accessible position just outside the box. The drive is direct on the top speed.

As can be seen from the admirable chassis staged at Olympia, the gear wheels are of excellent width and the teeth of stout design. On the rear of the primary gearshaft, where it issues from the gear box, we find an unusually wide brake drum, upon which heavy cast-iron flanged brake blocks apply. These blocks take effect on the drum by means of a rocking toggle arm, and can be immediately adjusted to the greatest nicety by simply turning a wing nut on the connecting stem. A neat universal joint is found on the forward end of the propeller-shaft, and at the rear, connecting up with the driving bevel wheel shaft, we find a non-torsional plunging joint of good design. The casing of this joint is saw-cut, and the joint made at the end of

the propeller-shaft by means of clip, stud, and bolt.

The Back Axle Design.

It would be difficult to conceive a more carefully-designed back axle than that occurring on this extremely well thought out chassis. The differential gear case is in aluminium in two vertical halves, and bolted to the right and left-handed sockets are steel tubes encasing the driving-shafts and carrying the bearings upon which the road wheels rotate. A steel centrally-strutted, V-shaped torque rod is carried in a vertical plunging standard attached to the tubular cross member of the frame already referred to, and radius rods adjusted by right and left-hand couplings, and fitted with universal joints (see sketch) at each end, where they attach to the frame and to the axle casing, are provided.

The side brakes on the back wheels are of the internally expanding type, the segments taking effect upon the interior peripheries of the brake drums of large diameter, forming part of the driving wheel hubs. The brake application fittings are of robust proportion, and a very neat form of compensation arrangement is found on the left-hand side of the brake striking sleeve.

We should have mentioned previously that the rear of the frame is strengthened by flat, rectangular-sectioned tie bars—a neater and better conceived arrangement than the mere use of channel section stuff. The rear of the frame is carried as shown by the sketch on stiff steel frame brackets and full elliptical springs of excellent design. All the wearing points of these springs are provided with force feed lubricators. This also applies to the front springs, which are of the semi-elliptical order.

The front axle is on somewhat unusual lines, but is without doubt of exceedingly strong design.

This remark also refers to the steering socket and steering pivots, while it is gratifying to find that the steering rod is placed above the steering distance rod behind the axle. The single fly in the amber of this extremely satisfying design is the slight bend in the steering rod, in referring to which. amongst so much that is good, perhaps we may be regarded as hypercritical.

There is no doubt that the chassis of the 15 h.p. Standard car is among the tit-bits of the exhibition.

Mr. Charles Friswell and the 20 h.p. Standard landaulet which he will use on his tour through India.

Apparently motor cars are not the only vehicles which exceed the limit. A L.C.C. electric car driver was fined £2 10s. and costs at Greenwich for covering a measured stretch at the speed of twenty-one miles per hour. which is by no means the best tram speed attained on London roads.

The New 15 h.p. Standard Car.

Bloc Engine, 79 × 114 mm. Three Speeds. Overhead Worm Drive.

Fig. 1.—Semi-plan view of the 15 h.p. Standard chassis.

FINDING a demand for a car of the 80 mm. class the Standard Motor Co., Ltd., of Coventry, have designed, and, after very thorough tests of the first few chassis turned out, have placed a model of this type on the market. This new model bears evidences of very careful design, and several unusual and practical features are embodied.

The engine is of the *en bloc* type, the bore and stroke being 79 and 114 mm. respectively. The crankshaft is very short and stiff, and carried on three bearings, which in their turn are carried from the top half of the crank chamber, so that the lower portion can be removed when necessary without disturbing the crankshaft bearings. The engine itself, together with the gear box, is supported on a sub-frame of considerable section.

The cooling water circulates by thermo-syphon. Four piston rings are fitted to the pistons, three above the gudgeon pin and one below. This fourth ring is fitted to ensure more efficient lubrication with less waste of oil, and is said to conduce to silent running of the engine. Inlet and exhaust valves are all on the near side, the distribution wheels in the front of

Fig. 2.—Off-side of the 15 h.p. Standard engine.

A, carburetter
B, throttle
C, minimum throttle stop
D, air intake

E, oil filter and distributer
F, crank chamber vent pipe
G, reserve oil tank

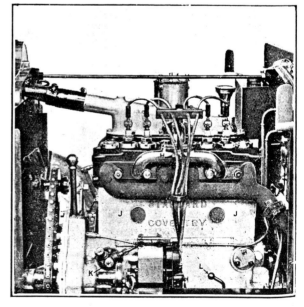

Fig. 3.—Near-side of the 15 h.p. Standard engine.

H, induction branch
J, valve spring covers

K, petrol pressure pump
L, handle of oil level cock

the engine being of large diameter and the teeth wide and of heavy pitch; the wheel on the crankshaft is of steel, while the half-time wheel driving the camshaft is built up of gunmetal and fibre to ensure quiet running.

The Bosch magneto which provides the ignition is also on the near side and driven off the half-time wheel by the shaft which at its front end drives the pulley for the radiator fan belt. The magneto coupling gives a very fine variation for adjustment of timing, the coupling itself being on the Vernier principle.

On referring to the photographs of the engine reproduced herewith, it will at once be noted that the carburetter is placed very high. This is in consequence of the desire to keep the induction pipe as short as possible, and in response to a colonial demand for the carburetter to be kept well up out of the way of water when fords and sluits are crossed. The principle also has the advantage of rendering the carburetter very accessible, and enables a peculiar system of heating to be adopted. From the sketch of this detail (fig. 5) it will be noticed that immediately upon leaving the carburetter the induction pipe passes through the water lead from the top of the cylinders to the radiator, the lead itself and the portion of the induction pipe passing through it being formed in one casting. Emerging from the water lead the induction pipe is then led direct to the valve chambers in the cylinder casting. The throttle is hand controlled by means of one of the levers over the steering wheel, and an adjustable minimum stop is provided. It will be

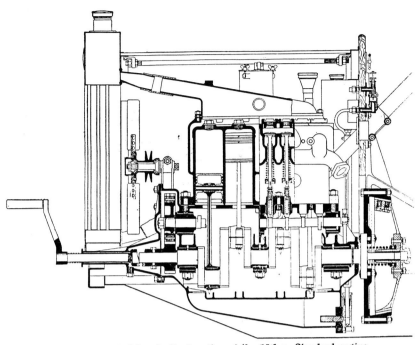

Fig. 4.—Vertical longitudinal section of the 15 h.p. Standard engine.

noticed in the sketch of the carburetter that immediately above the air inlet is a cross-shaft carrying at one end a lever and at the other end a short arm. The set screw forming the minimum adjustment stop normally butts against the head of this short arm. A small pedal is, however, provided between the clutch and brake pedals, which, when depressed, lifts the short arm so that the throttle can be rotated past the closed position to open a pure air inlet through which air can pass directly to the cylinders. Naturally, the carburetter being placed so high, a pressure-fed petrol system is fitted. Pressure is maintained in the tank. which is situated at the rear end of the frame, by a plunger pump directly operated by one of the exhaust cams. A gauge is provided on the dashboard to register the pressure maintained by this pump.

The lubrication system of this engine is somewhat unusual. The crank chamber is cast with a large sump below it, and in front of the dash inside the bonnet a

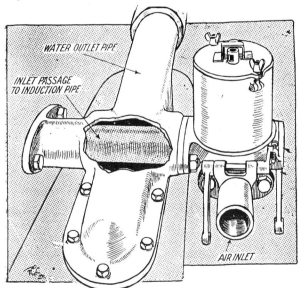

Fig. 5.—Sketch showing the position of the carburetter on the 15 h.p. Standard, and the manner in which the induction pipe passes through the water outlet from the top of the cylinders.

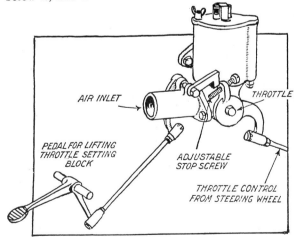

Fig. 6.—The arrangement of the throttle stop of the 15 h.p. Standard; the hammer-ended lever can be raised by depressing the pedal so that the throttle can be moved past the closed position, a pure air inlet then coming into operation.

reserve tank of oil is carried, so that on very long journeys the oil level in the sump can be maintained

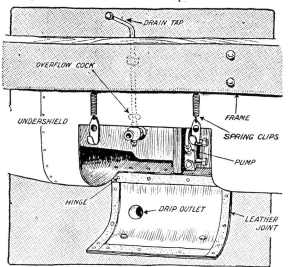

Fig. 7.—*The hinged opening in the undershield of the 15 h.p. Standard through which the oil pressure pump is easily accessible.*

by the operation of a control cock on the dashboard within easy reach of the driver's hand.

At the rear end of the single camshaft an eccentric is formed, which through a connecting link drives a direct acting plunger pump. This pump draws oil from the bottom of the sump and forces it to a filter and distributer piece mounted in a convenient position on the offside of the engine. From this point the oil passes through three leads to cups cast inside the crank chamber over the three main bearings. Small holes are drilled at the bottom of each cup through which the oil runs to the actual bearings. The amount of oil supplied by the pump is, however, far in excess of that needed by the bearings, consequently these three cups are always overflowing. That at the front end of the engine is so arranged that the surplus oil

runs immediately into the distribution gear case, lubricating the timing wheels and finding its way back to the crank chamber by a large hole in the partition. Cast with the false bottom of the crank chamber are four troughs in which a level of oil is maintained by that which overflows from the three cups previously mentioned. Into these troughs the connecting rod ends dip, throwing oil to the cylinders, pistons, camshafts, etc., as usual. A point claimed for this system of lubri-

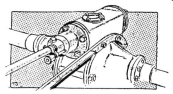

Fig. 9.—*The overhead worm drive of the 15 h.p. Standard; a portion of the built-up torque member is shown.*

cation is that it is entirely unaffected by any gradient which the car may climb or descend, for when ascending a hill the forward and centre cups overflow into the troughs, whilst in descending a gradient the centre and rearward cups maintain the supply. From all three sources the oil, after filling the troughs, overflows and passes through holes formed in the false bottom, so running into the sump again and being once more taken into circulation.

A point which should appeal to users in connection with the lubrication system is the fact that the wall of the crank chamber is drilled at four points, the holes so formed passing into the bottom of the troughs. Normally these holes are blocked by screw plugs, but these can be easily removed so that any deposit or dirt which may find its way into the troughs can be cleared out by means of a piece of wire or a small brush, such as a pipe cleaner.

The plunger pump which maintains the oil pressure is provided with a pressure relief valve, so that when the engine is started during cold weather the thick oil shall not generate too high a pressure in the system. The actual ball valve at the bottom of the plunger pump can be easily removed for cleaning purposes if required, for, as will be seen in one of the illustrations,

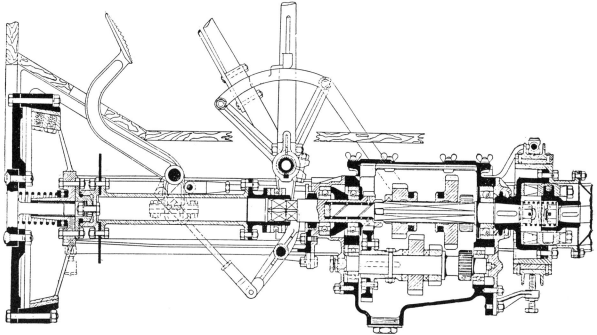

Fig. 8.—*The 15 h.p. Standard clutch and gear box.*

the under-shield is provided with a hinged flap which can be quickly lowered and so render the pump directly accessible. The oil sump is provided with a level indicator cock as shown in the sketch. A pressure relief pipe of large diameter is provided on the off side of the crank chamber, as will be seen from

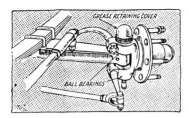

Fig. 10.—The swivel axle of the 15 h.p. Standard ; two journal ball bearings and one ball thrust bearing are fitted to each swivel.

one of the photographs, and through this the sump can be refilled. An oil pressure indicator is fixed on the dashboard, a small plunger being lifted by the pressure generated by the pump, so that the maintenance of the oil in circulation can be verified, the plunger being seen by day or felt by night.

Formed within the flywheel is an internal coned leather-faced clutch fitted with first engagement springs under the leather, an efficient clutch stop being provided to facilitate gear changing. Between the clutch and the gear box is a hollow connecting shaft with a square flexible coupling at each end.

The gear box is very compact, and provides three speeds and reverse manipulated by gate change. The mainshafts are carried on ball bearings, while the spigot bearing within the constant wheel is of considerable length and efficiently lubricated by holes being drilled through the constant mesh wheel at the bottom of several teeth. These holes pass through the boss of the wheel and the bearing within, the oil being forced through by the engagement of the teeth.

Many of our readers will have noticed that the gear wheels on practically all cars which show the most wear are those of the second speed. This is no doubt due to the fact that the change from top to second is the one most often made. Bearing this in mind, the designers of the car under review have made the second speed pinions of much greater width than those of the other speeds. Actually they are $1\frac{1}{16}$in. wide, and also of heavier pitch than usual. These two features taken together should undoubtedly conduce to longer life of the second speed wheels, a benefit apart from the additional ease of changing gear brought about by the use of the heavy pitch teeth.

Behind the gear box in the usual position the drum of the foot brake is fitted, an extension of the drum forming a cover for the universal joint at the front end of the propeller-shaft. The brake drum is very wide and thick, the brake itself being of the external variety. The universal joint at the front end of the propeller-shaft also provides for any plunging motion, whilst the joint at the rear end of the shaft is formed by the hexagon head of the shaft working in a hexagon cup. This rear joint is well encased and provided with a separate means of lubrication.

Worm drive has been adopted, although this system is by no means new to Standard cars ; an overhead worm is fitted, the ratio of the worm and worm wheel being $4\frac{1}{2}$ to 1.

The back axle casing is formed with an aluminium centre, this centre piece being built up in a somewhat unusual manner in three pieces, rendering the assembling or dismounting of the worm and worm wheel a comparatively easy job, the centre portion providing a solid abutment for the thrust bearings situated at each end of the worm. The aluminium centre carries tubular casings which extend to the spring and brake carriers at each end. The wheels are keyed to the tapered ends of the driving axles, but in order that the latter shall not take the dead weight of the car an extension of the hubs is carried within the ball races forming the outside journal bearings of the back axle. This feature of the design is apparent in the sectional drawing of the back axle reproduced on this page.

Special means of retaining the oil in the worm casing have been devised. A cast iron sleeve is mounted on each driving axle, and is held up by means of a coil spring against a long thick felt sleeve, which in turn abuts registering pins in the axle casing ; the cast iron sleeves thus revolve with the axles against the stationary felt packing, and being kept up to their work by the springs mentioned, form a self-adjusting oil gland.

The back brakes are of the internal type, cam actuated. An inspection hole is provided in each cover, through which the amount of wear which has occurred to the liners can be easily seen. No adjustment is provided within the wheels, for the cams are of such dimensions that before the end of the motion they provide is reached the time has arrived for the brake liners to be renewed. In order to take up lost motion caused at the brake lever by reason of wear of the liners a most accessible adjustment is provided underneath the floorboard of the driver's seat ; that is, in front of the levers of the compensating motion which ensures equal braking effect to both back wheels.

When inspecting this chassis we were pleased to notice that all the brake joints were encased in American cloth covers stuffed with grease and bound up securely. A similar method has been adopted with the steering

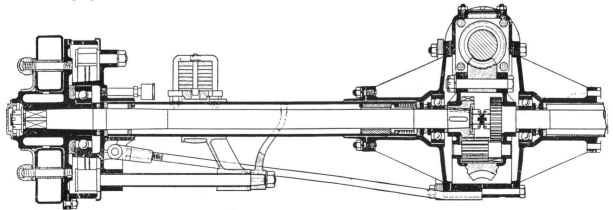

Fig. 11.—A vertical section of the 15 h.p. Standard back axle.

joints, a specially made leather cover being used upon every joint and secured with straps.

No radius rods are fitted, the front ends of the rear springs undertaking this duty, but a built-up torque rod with a hinging adjustable ball joint is provided.

Mention has been made of the rear springs, and attention is particularly directed to the care which has been devoted to the suspension of the chassis. All the springs are 2¼in. wide. At the front they are semi-elliptical in form, 3ft. long, whilst at the back a pair of semi-elliptic springs is fitted, each spring 4ft. in length, with the addition of two supplementary coil springs at each of the rear ends, which should add considerably to the comfort of passengers in the back portion of a four-seated body.

The steering worm and segment are both made of case hardened steel—a method which it is said provides much longer life than where a gunmetal or phosphor bronze segment is used.

One of the most carefully designed parts of the whole car appears to be the swivel bearings of the front axle ends, for the designers realise that a free steering is one of the most essential points tending to the full enjoyment of driving a car. Not only is a ball thrust bearing provided for each swivel, but at top and bottom of each centre pin is a ball bearing of large diameter. These bearings are protected from the ingress of dust by a system embodying the use of felt washers and closely fitting metal covers. The centre pin is provided with a transverse locking bolt as additional security in case at any time the swivels should be carelessly assembled. As previously mentioned, all the steering joints are leather encased in a very thorough manner.

Timken roller bearings are fitted to the front axles, while Sankey detachable wheels are provided at back and front. It may here be mentioned that each Standard chassis is sold complete with one spare wheel and tyre.

Two important dimensions of this car will be appreciated by colonial readers; the track is actually 4ft. 8in., and 10½in. road clearance is provided. Wheels, back and front, are 810 by 90 mm. The weight of the complete chassis is approximately 15 cwt.

The designers of these cars have not aimed at obtaining extremely high initial efficiency, but have had in view a design which will ensure the retention of a certain standard of that excellent quality, combined with reliability and smooth running. The good name which older models have earned is a proof of the wisdom of this policy, and the success with which it has been carried out. The design of the latest model bears evidences that no cheese-paring has been allowed; where the use of two classes of metal has been optional the more costly has been used if it were likely to be ever so slightly the better in the long run.

Rapid Revolution.
A Sleeve Valve Engine Test at 2,680 r.p.m.

It will be remembered that one of the criticisms levelled against the sleeve valve engine was that it would not run fast. Personally, we do not believe in running any engine at an exceedingly high number of revolutions per minute, though it is true that engine speed generally has gone up and continues to go up, and, of course, it is largely due to this increased normal speed that the comparatively small engines of to-day are doing work that, two or three years ago, much larger engines were required for. We can never believe that it is particularly good for an engine to be run at very high speeds, and there is also the fact that no engine is pleasant to sit behind when it is going really fast, say much above 1,500 r.p.m. One of the main reasons why we disbelieve in running the average engine at very high speed is on account of lubrication, as while it may be adequate for ordinary speeds it is a question whether it is sufficient when the engine is run fast and hard unless all the bearings are oiled under pressure. On the other hand, there is no doubt that many owners run their engines just as fast as they will go round, whether it be good for them or not, and we therefore thought we would take the opportunity of making a test of a 15 h.p. slide valve Daimler on a hill too steep for the legal limit to be exceeded, and at the same time well within the capabilities of the first speed. For this purpose we took the Sunrising ascent of Edge Hill which has a maximum gradient of 1 in 6.42, and over 900 feet of which are 1 in 8 or steeper. At this the car was put on the first speed, and instead of driving it as we should in the ordinary way with the throttle only partially opened and at a speed of ten to twelve miles an hour, we gave it full throttle, with the result that the speed went up to seventeen miles per hour, an engine speed of 2,680 r.p.m. We know this speed has been beaten frequently by engines specially prepared for racing purposes, but our little test was made with an ordinary standard engine and carburetter, and with a large five-seated body with two persons on the car and a full equipment of spares. It was quite sufficient to show that the sleeve engine will run at a very high rate of revolution indeed and do hard work at the same time, though, of course, when running at the speed mentioned it is no longer smooth or silent, nor do we know any engine that is. Again we should like to say to our readers that we do not advise running an engine so fast as a regular practice, and that the test we made was merely to ascertain whether the allegation we have referred to was justified or not—the only conclusion we can come to is that it was not justified.

A 17 h.p. Maudslay Colonial model which has just been shipped to Mr. W. Nelson, Waikoko, Hastings, Hawkesbury, New Zealand. This car has been fitted with a rough two-seated body, and will be used as a hack in a stud of some dozen and a half cars of different makes which Mr. Nelson and his family are at present using. Mr. Nelson is said to own the greatest number of motor cars and to be the largest breeder of sheep and cattle in the islands.

The picture above shows a 1912 six-cylinder Limousine, whilst at the other end of the scale, below is a Model 'S' Rhyl Tourer from the following year.

HEAD OFFICES

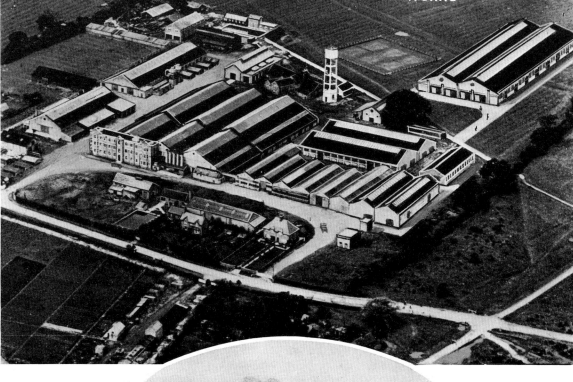

CANLEY
WORKS

TEST TRACK SHOWING THE
1 IN 4 GRADIENT

Introduction

WE believe that a study of the following pages containing the specifications and illustrations of Eleven and Fourteen H.P. 'STANDARD' Light Cars will bring conviction as to the merits of the design, the completeness of the equipment, and the outstanding value represented by each model.

There is, however, a limitation applying to any catalogue, no matter how elaborate it may be, due to the impossibility of describing by printed word, or illustrating by the reproduction of photographs, all the characteristics of 'STANDARD' cars which have won the unqualified approval of thousands of Owners.

After all, the real worth of a car to its owner and the satisfaction its possession and use afford are mainly, if not wholly, dependent upon its behaviour on the road, its riding comfort, its reliability, its economy and ease of upkeep, its durability, its roominess, the protection it provides in all seasons, and the " service " organisation behind it.

The pre-eminence in those respects of 'Standard' light cars accounts for their widespread and ever-increasing popularity among car owners, and for that reason we ask that they shall be judged, not merely by the printed particulars, illustrations and prices now put forward, but, in addition, by the opinions of users and by the enviable reputation they have secured among owner-drivers. If further evidence of their merits be required, facilities for personal inspection and trial of either model can be secured from us or from any of our numerous agents, who are to be found in all parts of Great Britain and in the majority of countries Overseas in which motoring is possible.

THE STANDARD MOTOR CO. LTD.,
COVENTRY.

The Standard
11 H.P. Light Car
R.A.C. 11·4.

ELEVEN H.P. CHASSIS (R.A.C. 11 4).

ENGINE. 4 Cylinder, 68 m/m bore × 90 m/m stroke (Rating 11·4 h.p.)

VALVES. Overhead, all in line.

LUBRICATION. Splash—oil being circulated by gear wheel on crankshaft to troughs.

IGNITION. Magneto.

PETROL SUPPLY. Gravity.

COOLING. Thermo-syphon.

CLUTCH. Disc type, metal driving plates engaging with flywheel, centre plate and clutch cover.

GEAR BOX. Three speeds forward and one reverse, R.H. gate change.

GEAR RATIOS. Top, 4·6 to 1; 2nd, 8·7 to 1; 1st, 20 to 1.

HAND AND FOOT BRAKES. On rear axle—both internal expanding, with renewable Ferodo Liners.

REAR AXLE. Underslung worm, ball bearings throughout.

FRONT AXLE. "H" section stamping, taper roller bearings in front hubs.

WHEELS. Detachable steel, 710 × 90.

TYRES. Dunlop, 710 × 90.

WHEELBASE. 8' 9".

TRACK. 4' 3".

GROUND CLEARANCE. 8½".

TOOLS.

Wheel Brace.
Open Ended Spanner, ⅜″ × ½″.
Open Ended Spanner, ⅛″ × ⅜″.
Tube Spanner, ⁷⁄₁₆″ × ⁹⁄₁₆″.
Adjustable Spanner.
Tommy Bar.
Screw Driver.
Combination Tool for Recess and Saw Cut Screws.
Tyre Pump.

Jack and Handle.
Valve Clearance Gauge.
Magneto Spanner.
Hammer.
Oil Can.
Pliers.
Sponge Cloth.
Petrol Funnel.
Carburetter Key.

File.
1 Hub Remover and Screw.
Tyre Levers.
1 Grease Gun.
1 Grease Nipple, ¼″ Gas.

SPARE PARTS.

Valve Spring.
Valve Collar.
Valve Cotter.
Valve Rocker Ball Pin.
One Dozen Assorted Nuts.
One Dozen Assorted Washers.
One Box Assorted Split Pins.

Carburetter Handbook.
Lighting Equipment Handbook.
Magneto Handbook.

The above lists are subject to alteration without notice.

Chassis Price - - - - £200

The 'Standard'
14 H.P. Light Car
R.A.C. 13·9.

FOURTEEN H.P. CHASSIS (R.A.C. 13·9).

ENGINE. 4 Cylinders, 75 m/m bore, 110 m/m stroke, monobloc casting (Rating 13·9), c.c. 1,944.

VALVES. All in line and enclosed.

LUBRICATION. Automatic—oil being circulated by a pump driven off camshaft and returned to a large sump.

CARBURETTER. Automatic.

IGNITION. High-tension Magneto.

PETROL SUPPLY. Vacuum fed from tank at rear.

COOLING. Thermo-syphon, large radiator and fan.

CLUTCH. Double disc type, metal driving plates engaging with asbestos covered surfaces on fly-wheel, cover, and centre driving disc.

GEAR BOX. Four speeds forward and one reverse, R.H. gate change.

GEAR RATIOS. Top, 4·6 ; 3rd 7·72 ; 2nd, 10·79 ; 1st., 19·85.

FOOT BRAKE. At rear of gear box ; external shoes and renewable liners.

REAR BRAKE. Internal expanding, shoes renewable.

BACK AXLE. Overhead worm, ball bearings throughout.

FRONT AXLE. " H " section stamping, roller bearings to front hubs and ball bearing steering swivels.

WHEELS. Detachable steel, 765 × 105.

TYRES. Dunlop Cord—765 × 105 m/m.

WHEELBASE. 9′ 8″.

TRACK. 4′ 6″.

GROUND CLEARANCE. 10″.

TOOLS.

1 Tool Box.
1 OpenEndedSpanner, ⅜″ × ¼″
1 OpenEndedSpanner, ⁵⁄₁₆″ × ⅜″
1 OpenEndedSpanner, ⁷⁄₁₆″ × ½″
1 Adjustable Spanner.
1 Double Ended Spanner.
1 Tube Spanner, ⅝″ × ⁹⁄₁₆″.
1 Tube Spanner for Gear Striker Screw and Oil Base Nuts.
1 ½″ Tommy Bar (Taper).
1 ¼″ Tommy Bar.
1 Magneto Spanner.
1 Hammer.
1 Pair Pliers.
Combination Tool for Recess and Saw Cut Screws.

1 Oil Can.
1 Petrol Funnel.
1 Sponge Cloth.
1 Carburetter Key.
1 Cold Chisel.
1 File.
2 Pin Punches (⅛″ and ¼″)
1 Comb't'nChamberCleaner
1 Pump.
3 Tyre Levers.
1 Detachable Wheel Brace.
1 Rear Hub Remover and Screw.
1 Jack.
1 Jack Handle.

SPARE PARTS.

1 Valve Spring.
1 Pair Brake Springs— Rear Wheel Brake.
1 Exhaust Pipe Packing.
1 Top Water Pipe Joint.
1 Hallite Jointing 6″ sq.
1 Soft Steel Wire, 6′.
12 Assorted Nuts.
12 Assorted Plain Washers.
12 Assorted Spring Washers.
12 Assorted C. & A. Washers.
1 Box Assorted Split Pins.
1 Grease Gun complete.
1 Grease Nipple, ⅛ gas.
1 Valve Collar.

1 Valve Cotter.
1 Gauge for Valve Clearance.
1 Special Screw Driver for Recess Screws.
4 Adjusting Plates Rear Wheel Brake.
1 Valve Rocker Ball Pin.

1 Carburetter Handbook.
1 Magneto Handbook.
1 Autovac Handbook.
1 " Standard " Instruction Book.
1 Oiling Diagram.

The above lists are subject to additions or deletions without notice.

Chassis Price - - - *India* **£325**

The 'Standard'
14 H.P. Light Car
R.A.C. 13·9.

THE "WARWICK" 5 SEATER.

14 h.p. All-Weather "WARWICK" Ordinary 5-Seater.

BODY - - - - Built of best ash framing. All doors fitted with slam grip type locks. Front seat fixed type.

TRIMMING - - - Cushions and squabs of best quality black leather, fitted with deep springcases stuffed with best hair. Pocket is fitted to each door.

HOOD - - - - "One Man" type, covered with black waterproof material.

CURTAINS - - - "Standard" Patent Side Curtains, made up with large celluloid lights, fitted to front and rear doors. Attached to the body by dropping into two bushes on top of each door, each curtain opens and closes with the door, and transforms the open car into an entirely closed vehicle. The curtains can be left up and used as side screens when the hood is down, and the rear curtains can be so arranged across the rear passenger's seat as to form a "V" screen, when required. When not in use, the curtains are carried behind the rear squab.

WINDSCREEN - - An adjustable sloping double windscreen is fitted, with holding-down pegs for hood, and rain gutter on the upper panel.

SCUTTLE DASH - Combines an instrument-board with large tray for parcels, etc. Finished natural colour Walnut.

PAINTING - - - Body highly finished in "Standard" Grey. Wings, bootings, etc., are painted black. All bright parts are heavily nickel-plated.

WHEELS - - - Detachable Steel.

TYRES - - - Dunlop, 765 × 105.

APPROXIMATE OVERALL MEASUREMENTS.—Length 13' 10", Width 5' 7", Height 6' 2".

Price - - - £375

EQUIPMENT.—Two-unit Lighting and Starting Set, including Head, Side, and Tail Lamps. Switchboard, Horn, Speedometer. Spare Wheel and Tyre. Full Kit of Tools and Spare Parts.

OPTIONAL EXTRAS.

Painting Blue Grey, Blue, Yellow, Crimson, Brown, or Green to samples supplied on request ... £8.10.0	Hood Cover... ... 2.10.0	Door to Tray on Dash 1.12.6
	Tonn' Cover in Twill 2.15.0	Rear Wind Screen ... 16.16.0
	Bulb Horn ... 1. 1.0	Luggage Grid ... 1.10.0
	Blind for rear window in Hood ... 10.6	Roof Lamp ... 17.6
Leather to choice of 6 samples, supplied on request 8.10.0	Special Carpets in rear to suit paintwork ... £1.10.0	Separate Adjustable Seats in front compartment, £10 per pair.
	Upholstery Covers in Poplinette ... 9. 0.0	D.N. Shock Absorbers £18.10 0 per set
820 × 120 Wheels and Tyres 10. 0.0	Mirror 17.6	Head Lamp Dimmer 1. 1.0

Subject to the Company's printed Terms and Conditions of Business.

'C O U N T   T H E M   O N   T H E   R O A D'

The 14 h.p. Standard at Moor Park

Few cars are more popular with the motoring golfer than the 14 h.p. Standard, which is here shown before the magnificent club-house of the Moor Park Golf Club. This car is neither sensational in design, nor freakish in appearance, but is a comfortable, economical vehicle, built to withstand hard and regular wear.

The 14 h.p. Standard in detail

The side screens on the Standard can be turned into an effective back screen that, coupled with the deep body, gives full protection to the rear passengers, even without the hood.

The 14 h.p. Standard on the road in the old-world village of Pinner. Note how the low line of the car gives very comfortable seating to the driver without in any way obscuring the full view of the road ahead.

A feature of the equipment is the detailed completeness of the side curtains. Here is shown how the side curtains, when being used as a rear screen, automatically release themselves when the doors are opened.

PART OF SAW MILL

SECTION OF BODY BUILDING

VIEW IN MAIN SHOP SHOWING TRACKS FOR ERECTION OF

SECTION OF FINISHING SHOP

PART OF FINAL TESTING DEPT.

SECTION OF BODY MOUNTING

SECTION OF PAINT SHOP

S.

CORNER OF DESPATCH SHOP

A BATCH OF STANDARD 13·9 4 SEATER CARS
SUPPLIED TO R.S. MURRAY & Cᵒ Lᵀᴰ FLEET WORKS, LONDON

The New 9.5 h.p. Standard.

Details of the Chassis and Coachwork of the 1919 Model Long Stroke Light Car.

SOME details of the 1919 programme of the Standard Motor Co., Ltd., of Coventry, have already appeared in *The Autocar*, in the issues of December 7th and April 5th. The first specimens of the completed design, embodying all the new features decided upon, were finished last week, when we had an opportunity of inspecting them in detail. Before doing so, we made a tour of the four works of the company, in order to examine the various parts as they progressed through the different operations. At the present time, the Standard works form a hive of activity, for 1,500 sets of parts are in hand, and erection on a quantity basis has begun.

Designed expressly for the owner-driver, probably no more popular type of light car exists than the one we are about to describe.

The latest edition possesses many improvements over the earlier examples, mainly noticeable in the points of convenience and the accessibility of parts requiring attention from time to time, such as one would expect from a factory, the *personnel* of the entire management of which are keen motorists themselves, and clearly make a study of the many details and improvements that go to make motoring enjoyable. Such a study of detail — unhappily too often overlooked—stamps a design "finished" or "unfinished," as the case may be.

The Standard Company never appealed to the competition driver; its most enthusiastic users are found among professional men, the class "over 40," as Mr. R. W. Maudslay, the managing director, aptly expressed it, and, after all, that class form the backbone of the motoring public to-day, just as they did yesterday.

The long wheelbase four-seater model, with hood and side curtains in position, forms an excellent all-weather car.

SPECIFICATION.

9.5 h.p., four cylinders, 62 × 110 mm. (1328 c.c.) monobloc casting.

Single disc clutch with asbestos on flywheel surface.

Three-speed gear box.

Overhead worm driven back axle.

Semi-elliptic springs.

Tyres 700 × 80 mm. on detachable steel wheels.

Wheelbase, 7ft. 8½in. Track, 4ft.

Ground clearance 9½in.

Electric lighting and starting.

A long stroke engine of 62 × 110 mm. has been adopted for this year after exhaustive tests extending over a period of several years, whilst its general performances have been comparable with other types of experimental engines which have been developed side by side in the Standard works. The increased cylinder capacity (1,328 c.c. compared with 1,086 c.c.) has provided just that additional amount of power which will win new appreciation for this already popular car. In general design the engine is much as before, the cylinders forming a *monobloc* casting, with the valves arranged on one side with separate valve caps, a special plug being provided at the opposite side of the cylinder to enable any carbon formation on the pistons to be removed without the necessity of disturbing the block casting. This is a praiseworthy refinement.

Perhaps the most noticeable features of the inside of the engine are the sound straightforward design and absence of "fancy" fittings. Two long white-metalled bearings support the crankshaft, whilst the shaft itself,

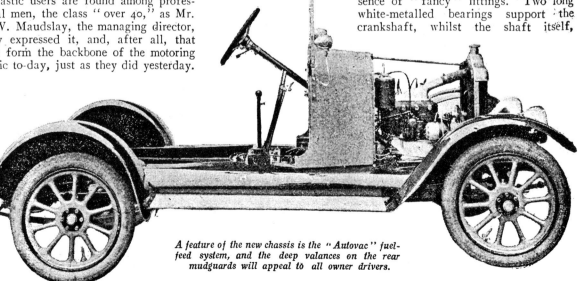

A feature of the new chassis is the "Autovac" fuel-feed system, and the deep valances on the rear mudguards will appeal to all owner drivers.

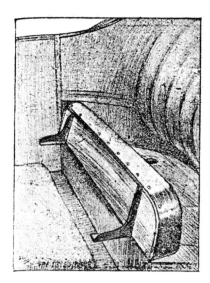

Front overhanging portion of seat is hinged to give easy access to the gear box and foot brake. The side curtains are carried behind the squab which lifts to give access.

which, incidentally, is set slightly *désaxé* to the cylinder bore, has been increased in diameter, and the amply proportioned big ends are each held by two bolts. Cast iron pistons, having two top rings are attached to the H section connecting rods by hollow gudgeon pins, and the plain-ended tappets form a simple and sufficient method of imparting the cam motion to the valves.

a simple means of adjusting the belt.

Aluminium bed plates, integral with the crank chamber, extend the full length of the engine, and not only protect the upper part of the engine from mud but also form rigid supports, by means of which the power unit is bolted to the frame, through the medium of wood packing strips.

Lubrication Details.

A gear type oil pump is driven directly from the tail of the camshaft. This

The oil filter is easily withdrawn on the new Standard.

Fuel is fed to the engine from a seven-gallon tank placed at the rear of the chassis through an Autovac installation placed just inside the bonnet, a horizontal type Zenith carburetter being employed to provide the mixture.

The triangulated distribution gear is quite a feature of the new Standard, and some interesting details are embodied in the layout. Both camshaft and magneto are driven by a single silent chain, and a micrometer adjustment is provided for the magneto timing. The magneto, with its driving-shaft and bearing, are assembled as a unit on an aluminium casting, and once the alignment has been checked at the works during the assembling of the car, there is no possibility of disturbing it. Adjustment for the driving chain is carried out by slacking the nuts which hold the magneto unit to the engine bed plate and tightening up a jack-nut between the casting and the crank case.

A Whittle belt drives a two-bladed aluminium fan and also the dynamo, the latter being placed on the near side of the engine and clamped in position by two bolts. The dynamo can be moved sideways on its bed plate by a draw bolt, and this provides

pump sucks oil from the oil base—which, by the way, is detachable from the lower part of the crank-case—and forces it through the camshaft bearings to the main bearings, and thence to constant level troughs, the overflow returning to the oil base. There are several interesting features in the lubrication system which are well worthy of mention, especially the thorough method of oil filtration. The suction pipe is enclosed in a gauze filter, and the delivery pipe leads directly to a second and easily accessible gauze tube, the oil finally returning to the sump through a perforated screen.

To prevent oil leakage through the dashboard circulation indicator, a very simple device has been introduced—for the indicator plunger is carried on the engine base, and its motion is transmitted to the dashboard by means of a light rod and bell crank lever. A bypass from the oil supply to the main bearings leads to the magneto shaft bearings, and a test cock is fitted just above this bearing, by means of which it is possible to ascertain at a glance if oil is flowing through the bearings or if there is any stoppage in the pipe system — an unlikely event in view of the fact that three filters are installed.

Power is transmitted through a single dry-plate clutch to the three-speed and reverse gear box by means of a short shaft having a flexible

The dashboard fittings, position of starting motor, speedometer drive, and seven-gallon petrol tank are shown in this rear view of the chassis.

C7

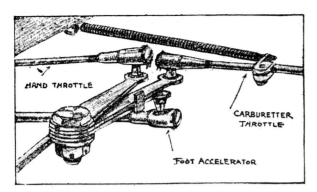

The hand and foot throttle control mechanism is somewhat unusual.

ring coupling at each end. The beds of the shaft are deeply forked so as to provide easy access to the large grease cup which serves the clutchshaft bearings and the castellations on which the clutch plate slides.

Both gearshafts are carried in ball bearings throughout, and the box, which has a detachable sump and well as cover plate, is carried on two angle-iron transverse members. The selector mechanism is composed of two shafts, each of which is positively locked when out of action, and is carried in the cover plate, an extension of which carries the gate quadrant and encloses the change-speed lever shaft.

Transmission : Brakes : Steering.

The transverse members mentioned above also support the Brolt starting motor, which is connected to the usual Brolt gear starter by means of a shaft with flexible joints at each end. This system introduces a convenient manufacturing proposition, for the gearing which is carried on the engine unit can be lined up correctly with the flywheel teeth regardless of the motor, and slight malalignment being taken up by the flexible joints.

Enclosed universal joints of the star type are employed at each end of the propeller-shaft, and an overhead worm drives the rear axleshafts. The practice of mounting the hubs direct on the outer ends of the axleshafts is retained, as it has given every satisfaction and has considerable advantages in providing wide bearing centres and simple design. Soft cast iron shoes are used in the rear wheel drums, the operating lever being bent over to a natural position for the driver's hand, and a simple toggle compensator is incorporated in the actuating mechanism.

The foot-operated fabric-lined contracting brake lies immediately behind the gear box. All brake ad-

In the two-seated open car the exterior lines make cleaning a simple matter.

c8

justments are placed in accessible positions, and an auxiliary adjustment is provided for the lower half of the foot brake.

Steering is by worm and wheel, and the steering gear is solidly constructed throughout. Incidentally, grease

The leather disc of the gear box coupling.

can be packed into the worm box through a particularly large and accessible filler, leaving the worm gear entirely submerged. The front axle is of exceptionally substantial design, and the steering heads and pivot pins have received all the attention which such very important items require. Both front and rear springs are semi-elliptic, those at the back being underslung and assisted by supplementary coil springs at the rear end.

Wheels and Bodywork.

Five Sankey detachable wheels are shod with 700 × 80 mm. tyres. A speedometer and electric equipment are supplied with both the two and four-seated models, the four-seated chassis differing from the two-seater only in that it is increased in length by one foot and shod with 710 × 90 mm. tyres.

The bodywork is full of interesting features, for, though both the two and four-seaters are designed as open cars, they can be converted into entirely enclosed vehicles which are as dry and draughtproof as though they were designed solely as closed carriages. Two piece adjustable windscreens are fitted, and the hoods are of black imitation leather. Patent side curtains fitted with large celluloid windows are contrived in such a manner that they open with the side doors and yet fit closely

The engine unit showing magneto position and triangulated belt drive for dynamo and two bladed fan. On the timing case there is an oil lead to the magneto-shaft bearing and test cock for oil circulation.

to the hood when the doors are shut. All the side curtains and fittings can be stowed neatly away in the squab.

The side doors are very wide, and the leg room is ample, while considerably increased accessibility is provided by the fact that the front portion of the seat cushion support is made to fold up, so that when the floor boards are raised a clear view is obtained of the propeller-shaft behind the foot brake. Similarly, in the two-seater model the folding dickey seats are so arranged that they can be entirely removed without undoing a single nut, so as to provide easy access to the rear axle and universal joint. This feature, which is carried out in a particularly ingenious manner, and in no way affects the rigidity of the dickey, is necessitated by the position of the petrol tank at the rear of the car, which would otherwise render the axle rather inaccessible.

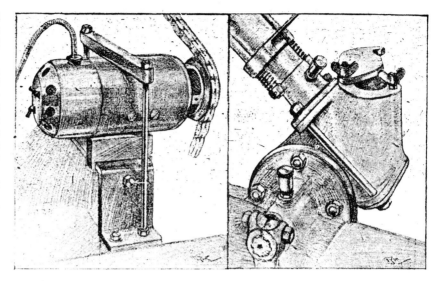

Method of mounting the dynamo and the adjustments provided. The convenient means of lubricating the steering gear box.

The design of the four-seater, which, by the way, is a four and not a five-seater, includes all the best features of the smaller model, and ample leg room is provided for the occupants of both front and back seats.

Considerable weight has been saved by the use of aluminium panelling, and the finish and upholstery are excellent.

Minor refinements which are yet of some importance are incorporated throughout the car, and amongst these must be mentioned the rubber buffers on which the radiator is mounted so as to insulate it from vibration, the fixings for the spare wheel, which enables two wheels to be carried side by side without the use of a well in the running board, and the tiny white lights in the side of the dashboard lamps, which are of great assistance when driving in narrow places.

One particularly attractive point of the bodywork is the provision of an open dash of really useful capacity in the space usually occupied by the petrol tank on small cars. In this goggles, map case, gloves, smoking accessories, and small parcels may be carried. The construction of the dash also renders the wiring of the electrical indicators particularly accessible, a point which is often overlooked by designers.

The new Standard is, in fact, a vehicle produced for the professional man and owner-driver, and, in spite of its roominess, comfort, and accessibility, it bears neither the appearance of clumsiness nor of being overbodied.

The price of the two-seater, with full equipment, is £350, but that of the four-seater model illustrated on page 846, has not yet been fixed definitely.

The Post-war Lanchester.

Modifications to be Embodied in a Striking Chassis.

A smart 40 h.p. Lanchester with clean design of four-seated body

ONE of the very few new type 40 h.p. Lanchester cars completed before the war is illustrated, and is in the possession of Mr. J. Cuthbert Jeffree, of Cardiff, and did much good work during the war.

Certain modifications will be embodied in the design of the 40 h.p. post-war model, but it can be stated that the chassis price has now been fixed at £1,500, which includes electric starting and lighting equipment, complete with five lamps, Dunlop or other similar priced tyres as desired, spare wheel and wheel carrier, spare tyre, speedometer, clock, two oil gauges, two electric meters, two complete separate ignitions, Rudge-Whitworth detachable wheels, bulb horn, complete set of tools, tool boxes, step-boards, and number-plates.

C11

Above, a 1921 "SLO" two-seater, and below, a four-seater Kineton Tourer based on the 1924 11.4hp "V3" chassis.

THE NEW 11 h.p. STANDARD.

A Thoroughly Equipped New Model at a Moderate Price to Take the Place of the 8 h.p. Car.

The car with its all-weather equipment in position. Electric starting, a 5-lamp lighting set, all-weather equipment, spring gaiters, and various other adjuncts, are included in the price of £250

APART from efficiency and refinement of running, the great feature of the new model Standard which will attract attention is the absolute completeness of the equipment as compared with the price. For £250 this new 11 h.p. car is to be sold complete with two-seater body and two-seater dickey, black hood, all-weather side curtains, double-panel windscreen, electric starting and lighting set with five lamps, spare wheel and tyre, speedometer, spring gaiters, tool kit, and a selection of spare parts.

In the main a revised edition of the recent 8 h.p. car, the new 11 h.p. vehicle is equipped with an engine of larger bore, namely 68 mm., has an improved worm and segment steering gear with a ball race under the steering wheel, and ball thrusts on the steering swivels of the front axle. At the back of the frame also an additional cross-member has been added. In the coachwork a body higher and wider by some four inches has been fitted, and this has nicely moulded sides, and a prettily curved boot, of which the single panel, when open, discloses a very roomy dickey seat. The back of the body is lined along the edges with a black beading, and the door is unusually wide, so that it is really easy to get in and out of the car when the hood is up—a point which will be appreciated

Excellent all-weather equipment in the shape of celluloid panels, with a minimum of fabric edging, is provided; these are easily put in place or detached, and the section above the door opens and closes with it. In the hood at the back an electric roof lamp is provided, whilst in the dashboard there is the useful shelf which forms a feature of Standard productions.

The four-cylinder *monobloc* engine has a detachable head and overhead valves in line, operated by unenclosed push rods and rockers. Cooling is by thermo-syphon, and lubrication by means of splash.

A magneto is used, and a Claudel-Hobson carburetter is attached to an inlet manifold combined with the exhaust. At the front of the engine is a belt-driven dynamo. Aluminium pistons are fitted. From the engine a single plate clutch conveys the drive through a fabric-jointed shaft to the three-speed gear box, the latter being mounted on the front end of the torque tube of the rear axle. The gear ratios are: Top 4.6, second 8.7, bottom 20, and reverse 15.8 to 1. The change speed lever is on the right-hand side of the car beside the brake lever, and both sets of brakes take effect on drums on the rear wheels. The six-gallon fuel tank is carried in the scuttle and feeds the carburetter by gravity.

In the course of a short trial of the new Standard we found the engine very lively. It can not only propel the car at a very satisfactory speed, but is flexible enough to allow it to be driven at walking pace on top gear. The steering is exceedingly light, and the springing and brakes decidedly good. The Standard car of 13.9 h.p. R.A.C. rating, previously known as the 11 h.p. Standard, will now be termed the 11-14 h.p. model

SPECIFICATION.

ENGINE: 11·4 h.p., four cylinders, 68 × 90 mm. (1,307 c.c.). Tax £12. Detachable head. Overhead valves.
TRANSMISSION: Single plate clutch. Three-speed gear box, underslung worm final drive.
SPRINGING: Quarter-elliptic back and front.
WHEELS: Detachable disc with 710 × 90 mm. tyres. Wheelbase, 8 ft. 9 in. Track, 4 ft.
PRICE: £250.

In appearance the new Standard is attractive. The body sides are higher than those of the earlier model of 8 h.p. which this model supersedes, and greater curvature is employed, together with a black beading round the edges. Ample leg room is also a feature.

CURRENT STANDARD CARS.

Some Features of a Wide Range of Attractive British-built Vehicles Suitable for Family Motoring. Excellent Saloon Bodies.

The 14 h.p. chassis accommodates commodious coachwork. (Left) The four-five-seater touring car is shown with its all-weather protection in position. (Right) The roomy " Pall Mall " saloon. Both types are fitted with balloon tyres.

IN relationship to pre-war days, the activities of a firm of the reputation of the Standard Motor Company, Ltd., are so very much greater in scope that there is a good deal of interest to be gleaned from summing these up. This year 10,000 Standard cars have been produced, and for 1925 it is the aim of the company to exceed those figures by some 35 per cent.—no small undertaking.

At the present time approximately two 11 h.p. cars are sold for every one of the 14 h.p. type. Of the 11 h.p. vehicles, about one in five is a two-seater, whilst the proportion with regard to the 14 h.p. vehicles is considerably less, which is what might be expected, in view of the fact that the 14 h.p. type is so eminently suited to a four- or five-seater family body that it would seem almost a waste of good space to employ it as a two-seater. One very marked feature about the demands of to-day is that the saloon type of car is becoming more and more popular.

Eleven Separate Complete Types.

Besides the bare chassis, eleven separate complete Standard cars, in two sizes of 11 h.p. and 14 h.p., are now being produced. Of the 11 h.p. type, there are five models ranging in prices from £200-£275, and of the 14 h.p. six varieties from £345-£475. Thus it will be gathered that there is a wide range of prices to suit most pockets.

Dealing first of all with the smaller type. The chassis has been in existence sufficiently long for its design to settle down for steady production, so that very little change has taken place of late. Before describing the various features of the coachwork, however, it will be well to touch briefly on the mechanical specification. The car is propelled by a four-cylinder engine (68 × 90 mm. = 1,307 c.c.), rated at 11.4 h.p., and taxable at £12. A block casting forms the cylinders and the upper half of the crank case, in which the crankshaft is carried in two bearings, whilst aluminium pistons and tubular connecting rods are incorporated. Overhead valves operated by push rods and rockers are employed, and the main lubrication system is a splash feed, the oil being circulated by a gear ring on the flywheel, and thrown into pockets and galleries feeding the main bearings and troughs beneath the connecting rod big ends. A double disc clutch, with the metal driving plates running in oil, connects the engine to the gear box, which is mounted on the forward end of the propeller-shaft tube. The box provides three forward speeds and reverse, the ratios being : Top 4.6, second 8.7, and bottom 20 to 1. It will be noted that this bottom gear is of a decidedly low ratio, so that very severe hills can be tackled with confidence.

Final drive is by underslung worm running in oil, and all the moving parts of the rear axle are mounted on ball bearings. Both hand and foot brakes take effect in unusually large drums on the rear wheel hubs, and are of the expanding type with asbestos-lined aluminium shoes. In design the front axle is normal, but the steering pivots are fitted with ball thrusts, and taper roller bearings are employed in the front hubs. Detachable steel wheels are fitted, and these are supplied either with Dunlop low pressure tyres, 27 × 4.40in., or with clipper cord tyres, size

POPULAR AND INEXPENSIVE.

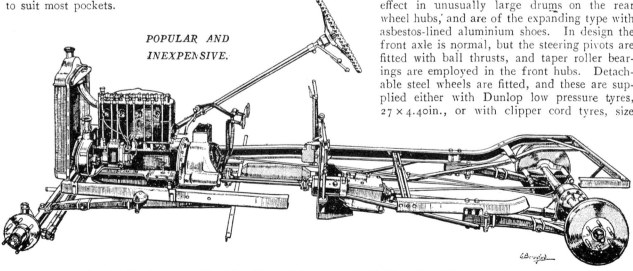

A part sectional drawing of the 11 h.p. Standard chassis, showing the disposition of the principal components.

16

B 25

Current Standard Cars.

710 × 90 mm. The wheelbase is 8ft. 9in., and the track 4ft. 3in. The chassis by itself is priced at £185.

Turning now to the complete cars, there are two ordinary models and two special ones. The first pair, a four-seater and a two-seater, known respectively as the " Kineton " and the " Coleshill," are priced at £200, whilst the special models are known as the " Canley " two-seater and the " Kenilworth " four-seater, priced at £235. The " Kineton " four-seater has a body built of steel panels, and is provided with three wide doors,

accommodation is in front, whilst there is a double dickey, which, when not in use, provides storage for luggage.

In type, the bodies of the special 11 h.p. cars, the " Kenilworth " four-seater and the " Canley " two-seater, are very similar to those of the less expensive vehicles, but aluminium panelling takes the place of steel. Either black or brown leather instead of leather cloth is used for the upholstery, and the hood is covered in black twill. Both the hood and the side curtains are of a better class. Special domed wings with valanced edges are fitted and the tyres are of a larger size (28 × 4.95in.) low pressure. Pockets are fitted in each door, and hair carpet is used to cover the rear of the front seat. Under the cushion of the front seat is a commodious well toolbox. In order to provide more foot room for the occupants of the rear seats, a channel is cut in the back of the front seats and a ramp board inserted.

COACHWORK ON THE 11 H.P. CHASSIS.

The 11 h.p. chassis is obtainable with widely differing coachwork to suit all tastes. (Top) The " Canley " two-seater, which has a double dickey seat. (Centre) The " Kineton " four-seater, with three-door body. (Bottom) The " Piccadilly " two-door saloon, one of the latest models to be introduced.

one on the left at the front, and two for the rear compartment. The front seat is fixed in position. The seats are upholstered in leather cloth, and both the cushions and the squabs have spring cases, and the one-man type of hood is covered in khaki waterproof material. In the front is a sloping two-panel windscreen, the top half of which has an adjustable swing, whilst in the scuttle is an instrument board combined with a tray for parcels.

All-weather Equipment.

A special feature is the all-weather equipment, celluloid side panels being built up on rigid metal frames. All the panels open and close with the doors, whilst that on the driver's side has a triangular flap for signalling purposes. The car is finished in brown with black wings and wheels, and the equipment includes the two unit electric lighting and starting set with two head lamps, side lamps, and tail lamp, electric horn, spare wheel and tyre, speedometer, spring gaiters, plain number plates, and full kit of tools and spare parts. The two-seater " Coleshill " model conforms closely in specification to the four-seater, excepting, of course, that the main seating

We come now to a type of car which is becoming very popular, and which is destined, we think, to become yet more of a favourite—the small four-seater saloon. The 11 h.p. Standard saloon is known as the " Piccadilly," and is priced at £275. It has two wide doors, and all its four windows are arranged to wind up or down whilst the handles to open the doors from the inside are placed well forward, where they can be reached in comfort. It is interesting to observe that, instead of the usual leather strap to limit the open position of the door, metal plates are employed, and are provided with spring buffers. Two separate front seats are fitted; that for the driver is adjustable, whilst the passenger seat is not only adjustable, but tips up and folds forward out of the way to give access to the rear compartment.

Features of the 14 h.p. Model.

The roof of the body, which is relatively high, is fitted with a lamp, and the plate glass windows are of considerable area, so that the interior is well lighted. This completes the 11 h.p. range.

Fitted with a four-cylinder engine (75 × 110 mm. = 1,944 c.c.), the 14 h.p. chassis is rated at 13.9 h.p., and the tax payable is £14. In detail the design differs

Current Standard Cars.

rather from that of the smaller car, for the block-cast cylinders of the engine are mounted on an aluminium crank chamber with three bearing crankshaft, H section connecting rods machined all over, and aluminium pistons. The cylinder head is detachable, and carries overhead valves operated by push rods and rockers, the rocker shaft being lubricated from the main oil supply induced by a

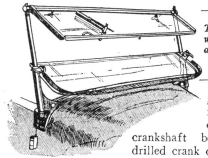

The latest design of windscreen with two adjustable panels on the 14 h.p. model.

gear pump which forces oil to the camshaft and crankshaft bearings, through drilled crank cheeks to the connecting rod big ends, and from gallery pipes to various other important points. A double dry disc clutch is employed, and the gear box, which is mounted on the cross members of the frame, provides four forward speeds with ratios —top 4.6, third, 7.72, second 10.79, and bottom 19.85 to 1.

The popular fabric type universal discs are used on the clutch shaft and also on the open propeller-shaft. On this car and also on the smaller one a right-hand change-speed lever is provided. Normally, two sets of brakes are fitted to the chassis, the hand brake consisting of expanding shoes in the drums of the rear wheels, whilst the foot brake is a transmission type operating on a drum at the rear end of the gear box. For the sum of £10 extra front wheel brakes can be fitted. These are of the expanding type, and are operated through cables; they are connected up to the pedal, and are used in conjunction with the countershaft brake.

Complete Two-Seater Models.

Dunlop low pressure tyres are fitted, size 30 × 5.25in., on detachable steel wheels, but 765 × 105 mm. cord tyres are optional. The wheelbase is 9ft. 8in. and the track 4ft. 6in., the price of the chassis only being £295.

Of complete two-seater cars, two types of " Leamington " are made, an ordinary model and a special. The first is priced at £345 and the second at £385. The difference between them is mainly one of equipment and

bodywork detail, whilst the more expensive car has larger tyres—size, 32 × 6.2in. Both cars have large double-dickey seats, the forward lid of which is adjustable to act as a scuttle, whilst on the special model a folding windscreen is fitted thereto. The hood has a single vertical support, and the rearmost side curtain can be left in place when the hood is down, being arranged to be independent of the latter.

Notable Side Panel Improvement.

Two types also are made of the " Warwick " five-seater, an ordinary model and a " special," priced again respectively at £345 and £385. In the special five-seater there are a number of interesting features to observe, the most striking being the arrangement of the side curtains. In this, the panels are spigoted into the doors in the orthodox manner, but one of the most notable advances which has been seen since celluloid side panels were first introduced, is now to be found in the way in which these new Standard curtains are arranged to act as sliding windows, the rear portion of each curtain being made so that it can be slid open or closed along horizontal rubber channels. Not only is this device exceedingly useful from the point of view of obtaining ventilation, but it is also perfectly neat.

"EXTRA AIR."

Small ventilators are placed beneath the scuttle and behind the valance to regulate the temperature of the front compartment.

Another point is the windscreen now fitted, which has the unusual feature of being easily and completely detachable. This is sloped, and both panels are adjustable, but the bottom one is hinged a little above its centre, so that it can be swung into a position to act as a baffle to cause air to flow downwards into the scuttle when the car is used in tropical climates. Further to expedite ventilation, controllable slots are provided at the bottom of the scuttle to draw the air out. The front seats of the car are built together, and together are adjustable over a wide range by means of securing links at the side. Provision is made at the back of the front

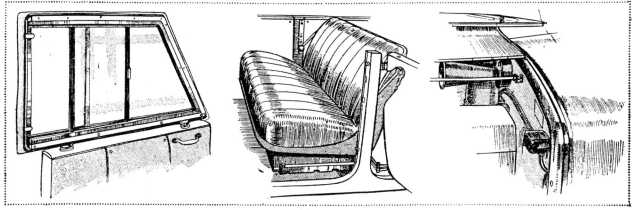

Three features of Standard cars are illustrated. (Left) The latest type of all-weather side panel, in which the windows are arranged to slide fore and aft for ventilation or signalling. (Centre) On the 14 h.p. model the front seats are adjustable fore and aft over a wide range. (Right) A little touch which will appeal to owner-drivers is the care taken to prevent bonnet rattle by the provision of a wide rubber pad in a channel round the front edge of the scuttle.

6   B 29

Current Standard Cars.

seats to carry a rear windscreen. The lower part of the back of the front seat is recessed out, and contains a toe board forming part of a tool box, the recess, of course, giving increased leg room to the back seats. Other points include the provision of a stout bracket supporting the steering column to the scuttle, an exceedingly rigid support for the spare wheel and a special arrangement whereby the back edge of the bonnet rests upon a lap of rubber instead of on the paintwork or a beading of the scuttle.

Of the saloon cars, the cheaper (the " Portland ") is priced at £375, and has a two-door body in style some-

A hand-operated air-scoop is provided to ventilate the front compartment of the 14 h.p. "Pall Mall" saloon.

what similar to that of the smaller Piccadilly saloon, which, by the way, personal test has shown us to be a very comfortable and excellently equipped body. The Pall Mall saloon, on the other hand, is a much more ambitious vehicle, priced at £475, and so many examples of it are to be seen about to-day that a description seems hardly necessary. It has a four-door body with four winding windows and a roof light for ventilation purposes, whilst on the scuttle there is an adjustable ventilator. The front seats are separate and adjustable. In appearance, the car is noticeable for its attractive straight lines and for the size of its windows.

QUICK-LIFTING DEMONSTRATION.
How the Sparklet Jack Makes Light of Raising a Heavy Rolls-Royce Car.

IN *The Autocar* of December 21st, 1923, we described the Sparklet jack, the latest pattern of which was recently entered for an official demonstration by the Sparklet Motor Jack and Televel Co., 39, Victoria Street, S.W.1.

The main body of the jack consists of a pressed steel cylinder of $3\frac{7}{16}$in. diameter, containing an indiarubber bag. Sliding in the cylinder, with its base resting on the bag, is a piston, the lifting of which raises the car. The handle of the jack forms a receptacle for a Sparklet bulb of a special size, the length being $6\frac{1}{4}$in. The rotation of the handle punctures the capsule of the bulb and admits gas to the rubber bag. A short handle is provided for use with smaller sparklets, and this, together with seven gas bulbs, is contained in the body of the jack. The weight of the jack with the short handle and six bulbs was 8 lb. $1\frac{1}{2}$ oz., and with the large handle 1 lb. more.

A jack was demonstrated on a 40-50 h.p. Rolls-Royce car with a front axle weight of approximately 19 cwt. and a rear axle weight of approximately 22 cwt. The size of the tyres was 895 × 135 mm., and the car was lifted from a deflated tyre. In the first test on the front axle it took 17s. to assemble the jack and locate it, while the actual raising of the car took $4\frac{2}{5}$s. In the second test the time for assembly and location was 26s., and for raising the car only 3s. In each case the wheel was lifted $5\frac{1}{4}$in. In two tests on the back axle the operations took 25s. for location and 4s. for lifting, and 16s. and $4\frac{2}{5}$s. respectively on the second test. The shortest time in which the jack was dismantled and a new bulb placed in position was 25s., and to lower the car 3s. was the shortest time taken. The car was left with the back axle on the jack for $16\frac{3}{4}$ hours, when it was found that the axle was the same height from the ground as when lifted.

OCCASIONAL SEATS.
Accommodating Extra Passengers in Comfort without Inconveniencing the Occupants of the Rear Seats.

IT is undoubtedly no easy matter to devise a satisfactory occasional seat. The number of such devices available is proof of this, and many of them are extremely ingenious.

It is essential that the occasional seat shall so fold away that it does not obstruct the interior of the car when it is not required, and at the same time it must be capable of being brought into use at a moment's notice. Furthermore, it must be strong enough to support the heaviest passenger likely to use it, and must provide a fair amount of comfort. It is in compromising between these various requirements that the difficulty lies in producing a satisfactory solution to the problem.

One of the latest Barker productions is the Empire occasional seat, which faces the direction of travel and is undoubtedly extremely comfortable. Owing to the manner in which the two rear legs of the seat are pivoted, it is rendered extremely rigid when in use, but at the same time it may be folded forward very easily, and then the panel at the back of the front seat—to which the Empire seat is attached—is hinged upwards, entirely

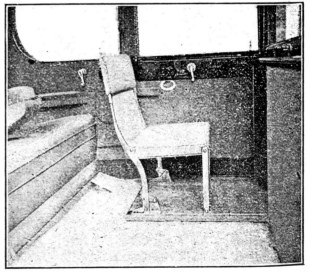

Folding flush when not in use, the Barker Empire occasional seat provides comfortable accommodation and does not in any way inconvenience the rear passengers.

concealing the occasional seat in the recess formed behind the panel. Owing to the clear space beneath the folding seat, ample leg room is allowed for the occupants of the rear seat.

B 30

A SOUND

Comfortable Suspension, an Excellent Body and Good General Performance Characteristics of the 14 h.p. Standard "Pall Mall" Model.

IT is generally acknowledged that there are few moderate-sized saloon cars more attractive in appearance than the 14 h.p. Standard with "Pall Mall" coachwork, and a recent trial of this car has convinced us that its attractions lie by no means only on the outside. In other words, the 14 h.p. Standard saloon comes very near the ordinary owner-driver's ideal of what a comfortable family car, with plenty of power and a really excellent body, should be.

The highbrow critic may find fault with various chassis details, but, after all, the proof of the pudding is in the eating, and the testimony of countless owners is that the 14 h.p. Standard goes, and keeps on going, in a manner which is probably the despair of the local repair shop proprietor. This, after all, is the outstanding quality that the average buyer demands in a car to-day. The Standard possesses it to the full.

It is easy to criticise certain of the mechanical details of almost every chassis, and the Standard is no exception to this rule. When, however, the criticisms of this chassis are carefully investigated, they are found almost invariably to refer to apparently rather crude, but essentially effective, methods of reaching the desired end. After all, if a very simple and inexpensive, though perhaps

Very wide doors are a feature of the car, as is the lightness of the interior, due to the generous window proportions.

(Right) A council of war. Discussing the wisdom of venturing along a flooded road at Shepperton.

B 16

21

FAMILY SALOON

a rather unsightly device gives perfectly satisfactory results, it is natural to ask : Why should manufacturers install far more costly, elaborate mechanism to serve the same purpose, and to serve it no better, in all probability?

We may, therefore, fairly dismiss almost all the criticisms advanced in connection with the Standard chassis, and say definitely that it is a thoroughly sound, reliable job that will give first-class service to its owner over a long period of time.

A Fine Saloon.

Not even the most captious critic is likely to find fault with the bodywork of the "Pall Mall" saloon. It is an admirable body, very comfortable, and fitted with all the contrivances and conceits regarded

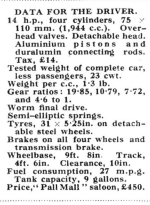

DATA FOR THE DRIVER.
14 h.p., four cylinders, 75 × 110 mm. (1,944 c.c.). Overhead valves. Detachable head. Aluminium pistons and duralumin connecting rods. Tax, £14.
Tested weight of complete car, less passengers, 23 cwt.
Weight per c.c., 1·3 lb.
Gear ratios: 19·85, 10·79, 7·72, and 4·6 to 1.
Worm final drive.
Semi-elliptic springs.
Tyres, 31 × 5·25in. on detachable steel wheels.
Brakes on all four wheels and transmission brake.
Wheelbase, 9ft. 8in. **Track,** 4ft. 6in. **Clearance,** 10in.
Fuel consumption, 27 m.p.g.
Tank capacity, 9 gallons.
Price, "Pall Mall" saloon, £450.

as essential by the modern owner-driver and his wife. The car has a very fair turn of speed, the normal maximum being in the neighbourhood of 47 m.p.h., though in favourable circumstances 50 m.p.h. and even a shade more can be touched.

Acceleration, though not outstanding, is quite good enough to satisfy all reasonable drivers of this class of car. From a steady speed of 10 m.p.h., an increase to 30 m.p.h., using top gear only, takes sixteen seconds, while by using second and third gears this time can be reduced to 11½ seconds. For handling in traffic, the Standard can be thoroughly recommended ; despite its four wheel brakes, the turning circle of 40ft. enables it to be turned without reversing on a fairly wide main road—a good trait in a town car.

Good Suspension.

In one very important point the latest 14 h.p. Standard is immensely better than its forerunners. We refer to the suspension, which in earlier models was sometimes apt to be on the harsh side, resulting in considerable fore-and-aft pitching over certain classes of road surface. The car is now fitted as standard with Smith

A Sound Family Saloon.

shock absorbers, which, together, doubtless, with improved springs, has transformed it into a really well-sprung, comfortable car. When long journeys have to be undertaken, the question of suspension is for many people of very real concern.

The Standard should rank high with that not inconsiderable section of the motoring public which regards gear changing as a penance to be avoided whenever possible. Owing, probably, to the lightness of the clutch spinning member, the four forward ratios provided by the gear box can be engaged without the slightest difficulty, and, incidentally, without double-clutching, though, of course, in that case a perfectly silent change down cannot be made at anything above quite low speed. If the double-clutch method is adopted, as it should be on all cars, there is no easier gear change.

A Matter of Entry and Exit.

Both gear and brake levers are on the driver's right-hand side, and here we have a criticism to advance. It is that an effort should be made to render exit by the wide door on the driver's right more easy than it is at present. By moving the gear lever and gate only a few inches further forward, the desired end could be achieved.

The front seats are independently adjustable, though to effect an adjustment a spanner must be used, while the angle of the back seat provides great comfort for the occupants of the rear compartment. While on this subject we may fairly congratulate the makers of the car, the Standard Motor Co., Ltd., Coventry, upon the excellent quality of the leather upholstery used for both front and back seats.

So far as hill-climbing is concerned the car can be thoroughly recommended. All average main road hills can be taken at a good touring speed on top gear, while it is seldom that on a main road anything calling for a change below third is encountered. Starting from rest can be easily performed on second speed, while first may be regarded in the light of an emergency provision.

We were decidedly impressed with the capabilities of the four wheel brakes. They are not in any way sensational when used in the normal manner, though, if the driver seriously gives his mind to the problem of a quick stop, it can be achieved in a remarkably short distance.

Excellent Brakes.

What is particularly attractive is the smooth manner in which the car is slowed and stopped in normal conditions. The pedal actuates the front wheel brakes and also a brake on a rearward extension of the gear box driven shaft, while the hand brake actuates shoes in drums on the rear wheels. All brakes are compensated, and adjustment is adequate, though not too accessible. In this last-named respect an improvement could probably be made without much difficulty

Women drivers, particularly, will be charmed by the lightness of the clutch. True, it is not often required, but a light clutch is a great asset in dense traffic.

The steering is beyond reproach, and, even with 31 × 5.25in. balloon tyres, the operation is easy, not only at touring speeds, but also at a mere crawl.

Reverting to the saloon body, all the windows are operated by winders, and what is practically equivalent to an open car with the hood up can be achieved in a moment when weather conditions suggest that a closed

car is not required. The instrument board is divided in the centre by a capacious cubby hole, very useful for the accommodation of the smaller impedimenta required in touring or on shopping expeditions. Two excellent dash lamps are available, and a roof lamp is also a standard fitting. Another praiseworthy feature is the roof ventilator, adjustable to any opening desired.

A word of praise must also be given to the C.A.V. electrical installation. Not only are the lamps genuinely

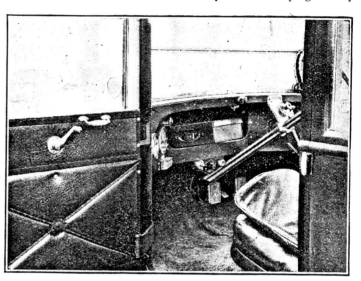

In the particularly capacious dashboard cubby-hole there is ample accommodation even for quite large attaché cases. On the steering column bracket will be seen the head light dimming switch, and beside it the carburetter air strangler. Beneath the cubby hole are mounted, from left to right, the oil indicator, engine starter switch, and ignition switch.

effective, but the starter deals quite contemptuously with the engine even on a cold morning. We had occasion three times to start the engine from cold with a temperature in the neighbourhood of freezing, and the combination of C.A.V. equipment with a Zenith carburetter, provided with an air strangler operated from the dash, resulted in steady firing on about the third or fourth turn of the crankshaft.

A suction-operated windscreen wiper is a standard fitting. As one small indication of the thoughtfulness of the Standard coachwork designer, it may be mentioned that the cocoa-nut fibre mat for the driving compartment has a detachable section, easily renewable, where the driver's left heel normally rests when operating the clutch. Every driver knows how soon this spot shows wear.

Well Conceived Details.

Lubrication of the chassis is by grease gun, and the tool accommodation is fairly generous. The spare wheel is carried at the back of the body, just in front of the folding luggage carrier. Three of the four wide doors have internal locks, while the fourth is provided with a Yale type lock, so that when all the windows are raised the car may be left safely without risk of loss by pilfering. Incidentally, with this arrangement and the hand brake applied, the car cannot be moved about in a public garage.

To sum up the whole matter, the 14 h.p. Standard "Pall Mall" saloon is a thoroughly pleasant car to drive, capable of taking a full load over any reasonably practicable country, with entire satisfaction and every comfort for the driver and passengers.

A "TWELVE" WHICH APPEALS.

Notes on the Construction, Equipment, and Road Performance of the Latest Type 12-24 h.p. Standard Saloon.

DATA FOR THE DRIVER.
12–24 h.p., four cylinders, 75 × 110 mm. (1,944 c.c.). Push rod operated overhead valves. Detachable cylinder head. Tax £14.
Tested weight of complete car less passengers, 1 ton 3 cwt.
Weight per c.c., 1·3 lb.
Gear ratios, 18·4, 8 05 and 4·6 to 1.
Final drive overhead worm.
Semi-elliptic springs
Tyres 28 × 4·95in. on detachable steel wheels.
Brakes on four wheels.
Wheelbase 9ft. 4in. Track 4ft. 8in.
Tank capacity 6 gallons. Consumption 25 m.p.g.
Price, Saloon £335.

WHEN one considers that in the year 1914 a 12-15 h.p. four-seater saloon class of car cost in the neighbourhood of £600, it is quite amazing to realise that in 1926 a much-improved saloon of such size as the new 12 h.p. Standard costs, with every conceivable form of equipment and a more refined road performance, only £335. Moreover, the price of the new car includes four wheel brakes, five-lamp electric lighting set, low pressure tyres, automatic windscreen wiper, luggage grid, and adjustable front seats, to mention just a few of the items which in the old days were either unobtainable or regarded as extras.

Introduced initially at the last Olympia Show, the 12-24 h.p. Standard now in production has been slightly modified in the interim, and we have recently inspected and made a road trial of the latest type, the model chosen being the four-five-seater "Park Lane" saloon.

Smart Exterior; Comfortable Interior.

Saloon cars are obtaining a steady increase in popularity, and it is very interesting to examine in detail the general scheme and equipment of one which is so moderately priced as the Standard.

Decidedly attractive in outward appearance, with a sloping windscreen and curved panels at the back, the body has four wide doors, in each of which is a winding glass window. Wide fixed windows illuminate the rear of the sides, whilst in the back panel is a window of considerable area provided with a spring roller silk blind. Smartly upholstered in fawn cloth, the interior is inviting, for the separate front seats, of the flexible back bucket type, are adjustable fore and aft, and have also tilting backs. Deep and softly upholstered, the rear seats are comfortable, there is sufficient leg room, and the provision of an adjustable ramp board, which when opened provides an extra toolbox, is a wise one.

Underneath each cushion of the front seats, by the way, is also a locker for tools and spares. Over the rear compartment in the roof of the car is an adjustable ventilator and also a rack to carry hats or light parcels.

Equipment for All the Year Round.

The front of the body terminates in a polished instrument board in which is a shelf of considerable size with a net front, whilst before the driver are grouped the following instruments : thumb-screw control for an adjustable ventilator in the scuttle, oil gauge, starter switch, clock, speedometer, electrical instrument board, dash lamp, air strangler for the carburetter, and electric horn button. Horizontally divided, the sloping front windscreen has an adjustable top panel with screw cramp locks to prevent rattle, a driving mirror in the centre, and a Lucas automatic screen wiper. At the back of the car is a strong luggage grid, upon which the spare wheel is carried in such a way as to be below the grid when the latter is open. On the right-hand running board is mounted a spare 2-gallon petrol tin, and on the left is the accessible Lucas battery.

Thus it will be seen that not only is comfort catered for, but that the equipment included with the car is wide

While retaining the characteristic lines, the radiator of the 12-24 h.p. Standard is bow-fronted and neatly enclosed at the sides. Four wheel brakes and Hartford shock absorbers are part of the equipment.

A " Twelve " which appeals.

enough to embrace every possible form of motoring contingency from town work in the winter to touring in the summer. Forethought is extended even to the tools, the jack has a double head so that it can be slid underneath the front axle as easily as the rear, and the wheel brace is of the magazine type, which collects the nuts, whilst it unscrews them and holds them ready to be replaced.

To ensure rigidity, the four-cylinder engine is of the type where the cylinder block and the upper portion of the crank case are formed in a single iron casting with a detachable cylinder head, in which are overhead valves operated by push rods and rockers and lubricated directly from the pressure oil system.

(Below) Neatness characterises the four-cylinder overhead valve engine. The magneto is driven in tandem with the dynamo, and at the back of the fan a water impeller is fitted.

Three bearings support the crankshaft, and aluminium pistons are used. The dynamo is mounted on the left side of the crank case and is positively driven, whilst in line with it is the magneto. The electric starter is mounted at the back of the engine and engages a gear ring on the flywheel. At the front a belt drives the fan, and a continuation of the spindle of the latter drives a water impeller which assists the water circulation. The inlet and exhaust manifolds are attached to the right side of the cylinder block, where the Zenith carburetter also is mounted.

Gear Box and Brakes.

Pressure lubrication of the engine is provided by a plunger pump driven off the camshaft. Besides a dipstick to show the level of oil in the sump, there is also a maximum level cock, whilst with the lip-stick is incorporated a whistle which sounds in order to give automatic warning if the sump should become empty of oil to a dangerous level.

Between the engine and the gear box is a double disc clutch, having metal driving plates. From the three-speed gear box, which has a right-hand control, the drive proceeds to the overhead worm-driven rear axle through an open propeller-shaft with fabric joints. Behind the gear box, by the way, is a contracting type band brake operated by the side lever. The four wheel braking system is operated by pedal, and the adjustment intended is that the front wheel brakes should do 60 per cent. of

the work and the rear wheel brakes 40 per cent. Hartford shock-absorbers are fitted to both front and rear axles, also gaiters on the springs. Grease gun chassis lubrication is provided.

The two-litre engine is well up to the work required of it. The car has a maximum speed on top gear in the near neighbourhood of 50 m.p.h. and will reach 31 or 32 m.p.h. on second. On a level road it can be accelerated from 10-30 m.p.h. on top gear in 17s. and on second

(Above) Separate and adjustable front seats with tilting backs are employed, and the ramp for the rear seats is also adjustable.

gear in 13s., whilst using second and changing into top at 25 m.p.h. the time taken to increase the speed between the limits mentioned was 14⅕s. These figures were obtained with three people on board.

Like many cars, the 12-24 h.p. Standard has a particular range of cruising speed where the whole car runs in harmony and is pleasantly smooth and quiet. This speed lies between 35-40 m.p.h. At the lower ranges of speed on top gear, especially under acceleration, the engine betrays the fact that it is at work, but cannot be termed harsh.

Behaviour on Hills.

Various main road hills were tackled during the course of the test. Frizz Hill, close to Compton Verney in Warwickshire, was climbed, the greater part of the way on top gear, finishing on second at 20 m.p.h. Edge Hill, between Warwick and Banbury, was approached on top gear at 40 m.p.h., a change into second was made at 30 m.p.h. opposite the warning sign close to the foot, the greater part of the hill was climbed at 20 on second, dropping to 12 m.p.h., and a change into bottom gear at 10 m.p.h. for the steep part at the summit. Sunrising Hill, between Stratford and Banbury, necessitated second gear on the first slope at 30 m.p.h., 25 m.p.h. up to the right-hand corner, 15 m.p.h. round the corner, and a change into bottom gear up the steepest part at 9 m.p.h. Warmington Hill, on the Warwick-Banbury road, was a comfortable climb on second gear at 20 m.p.h.

From the point of view of the driver the car is easy to handle; both the clutch and the brake pedal have somewhat longer travels than usual, but the clutch, and, indeed, the controls generally, are light to operate. Placed on the right side and set far enough back to come very conveniently to the hand without stretching, the gear lever is incidentally sufficiently far back to limit somewhat the range of adjustment of the driver's seat. The lever is short and easily moved, whilst the gear change itself is a very easy one to handle. Under the steering wheel are controls for the throttle and ignition, the steering itself is light and direct, and practically unaffected by road inequalities. The shock-absorbers, combined with flat springs, render the suspension of the car good, and the hold of the road what it should be; pitching and rolling are absent.

As regards the brakes, the four wheel set will draw the car up to a standstill on a level road from 40 m.p.h. in 118ft. We found it possible to bring the car rapidly to a dead stop from coasting at 20 m.p.h. down a gradient of 1 in 6 with the exertion of a fair amount of force on the pedal.

One other point—the whole car, indeed, is of a practical nature—is that the head lamps are carried on a horizontal stay which supports the front wings, and are arranged so that they are adjustable. They can, if necessary, be tilted considerably downwards for driving in fog. The 12-24 h.p. Standard Saloon is an excellently equipped and comfortable car, well arranged, and possessed of a sound road performance.

A SMALLER WILLYS-KNIGHT "SIX."

Luxurious Appointments and High Performance are Features of the 21 h.p. Model now Introduced to this Country.

Symmetrical and well-proportioned coachwork lines characterise the new 21 h.p. Willys-Knight saloon.

ALTHOUGH the big six-cylinder Willys-Knight is well known and widely appreciated (a test run was described in *The Autocar* of April 16th), its smaller edition has only just been introduced to this country.

Known as the "Model 70," this car has a Knight sleeve-valve unit, with a seven-bearing crankshaft similar to that of the larger model. The bore and stroke, however, are 58.7 × 111.1 mm., giving a total capacity of 1,842 c.c. and a Treasury rating of 20.7 h.p. The dimensions of the chassis are smaller generally, the wheelbase being 9ft. 5¼in., and the frame is correspondingly lighter, having a depth of 4½in.

Handsome Exterior; Comfortable Interior.

Transmission and brake lay-out are similar, except for the Borg and Beck single dry-plate clutch, which replaces the multi-plate component on the large car. The gear ratios are 5.11, 9.1, and 16.1 to 1, unit assembly of the gear box being adopted. The tyres fitted are 30 × 5.25in.

Externally, the engine is remarkably neat, and the auxiliaries are commendably accessible. The engine differs from that fitted to the larger model in that the exhaust manifold is taken round the front of the cylinder block to the near side, and then passes to a muff surrounding the induction pipe. The whole of the exhaust heat is available, therefore, for warming the incoming gas, adding greatly to carburation efficiency.

The Tillotson carburetter is fed from a Stewart vacuum tank, and the air intake is protected by a filter. A feature common to all Willys-Knight engines is the interconnection between the throttle and the by-pass valve in the lubrication system, whereby, as the throttle is opened, the oil pressure is raised.

The silence and sweet running of the sleeve-valve engine lend themselves particularly to the use of enclosed bodywork, and a full five-seater coach is standardised. In detail, the bodywork compares favourably with that of the larger car, being roomy and well finished. The interior height of the saloon is 45¼in., and from the pedals to the back rest of the driving seat there is a clear space of 36in., while from the back of the front seat to the rear seat back rest measures 38in. Ample room for three persons is provided by a width of 45½in. across the rear seat. The overall length of the car is 13ft. 5in., the height is 6ft. 1¼in., and the width 5ft. 5½in.

Top Gear Performance.

As a top gear performer the car is no less remarkable than its bigger prototype. On a climb of 1,200ft. in a distance of about two miles, with numerous sections of 1 in 8 gradient, and several short stretches of 1 in 6 to 1 in 4¾, second gear was not required for more than 300 yards, and it was amazing how even on 1 in 8 to 1 in 7 gradients the engine would slowly pull its load in a manner reminiscent of a steam engine. On top gear a speed of just over 60 m.p.h. was attained on a level stretch of road.

The brakes—internal expanding on the front wheels and external contracting on the rear—are smooth and powerful. The five-door five-seater saloon is priced at £495, and the five-seater open touring car is available at £395.

15

B 19

The 9 h.p. Chassis

£165

9 H.P. CHASSIS SPECIFICATION

ENGINE.   Four cylinder, 60 m/m bore, 102 m/m stroke, R.A.C. rating, 8.9. h.p. 1155 cc.   Tax £9.

Valves.—Side by side valves, inlet being larger than exhaust ensuring maximum power.   Exhaust valves in stainless steel.

Crankshaft exceptionally stiff, two-bearing type, $1\frac{3}{4}''$ diameter front main bearing, $2\frac{1}{4}''$ diameter rear, $1\frac{3}{4}''$ diameter big end.   All bearings bronze white metal lined.   Crankshaft carefully balanced on "Gisholt" machine.

Pistons—split skirt aluminium type, do not "slap" and cannot seize.

Connecting rods in duralumin, reducing loads on big end bearings and giving exceptional smooth running.

Cylinder head detachable, great attention has been paid to water flow round exhaust valves ensuring maximum efficiency of Thermo-Syphon cooling.

Lubrication—pressure system throughout by gear pump, very accessible, oil passages integral with cylinder block, no piping, relief valve fitted.   Oil filler very accessible and float to indicate level.

Electrical equipment—12 volt two unit system, dynamo and magneto being very accessible.

Auxiliary drive to camshaft and dynamo by chain with easy means of adjustment.

Ignition by magneto having variable timing.

Carburettor—Zenith horizontal type, very accessible.

CLUTCH.   Single dry plate type, exceptionally light driven member facilitating gear change, toggle type withdrawal gear, withdrawal sleeve mounted on extension of gearbox avoiding any possibility of friction on clutch shaft.

The 9 h.p. 'SELBY' Four-Seater

The 9 h.p.
'SELBY' Four-Seater

SPECIFICATION.

Oil pump very accessible, can be removed without breaking any pipe connection.

Body framed in ash. Panelled in steel. Seats comfortably four adults, the front seat being adjustable. Four wide doors. Folding head with efficient side curtains, which can be retained in position when the hood is folded down. The front side curtains have a hinged panel for signalling. The side curtains, when not in use, can be stored behind the rear squab. Body finished in cellulose. Choice of three colours—Red, Blue, Fawn. Adequate mudguarding. Complete with five wheels and tyres.

£190

Wire Wheels, **£10** extra.

Triplex glass can be supplied at an extra charge.

Dual colour paintwork, as illustrated on Two-Seater, in Grey and Blue, Fawn and Crimson, Vermillion and Crimson, £3 3s. extra.

Overall dimensions : Length, 11′ 4″. Grid down, 12′ 1½″. Width, 4′ 9″. Height, 5′ 10″. Approximate weight, 15 cwt.

Timing chain adjustment very easily carried out by slacking off 4 nuts.

EQUIPMENT.

Luggage Grid, Driving Mirror, Speedometer, Clock, Dash-Lamp, Petrol Gauge, Automatic Screen Wiper, 12-volt Electric Starter and 12-volt Lighting Set with Five Lamps, Centrally Grouped Illuminated Instrument Board, Electric Horn, Licence Holder, Plain Number Plates and Full Kit of Tools and Spares.

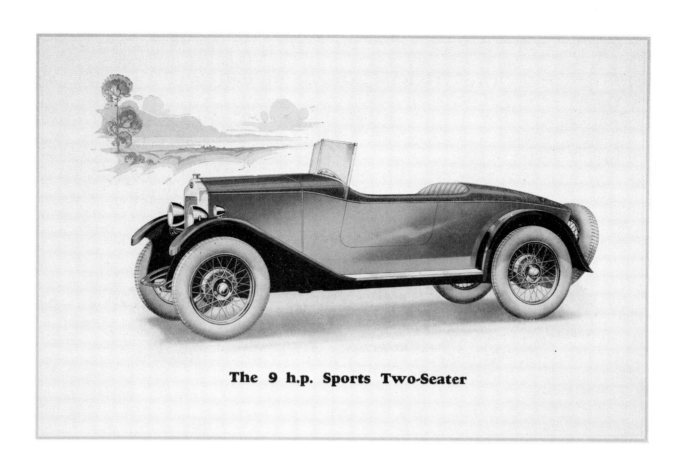

The 9 h.p. Sports Two-Seater

The 9 h.p. Sports Two-Seater

Metal Universal Joints with oil tight covers. Provide smooth transmission, a great improvement over the fabric joint.

Of "racy" appearance, the deck and sides being in different colours, comfortable seating for two, luggage space at rear concealing hood and fittings, fabric covered sides, the whole being of extremely light but rigid construction. V type windscreen. Wire wheels and shock absorbers standard. Guaranteed speed 60 m.p.h. Colour—Sides and wings, Blue ; deck, Aluminium.

£225

Supercharged model, guaranteed speed, 75 m.p.h.
(Engine 60 m/m × 97 m/m = 1097 c.c., optional)
£75 extra.

Triplex glass can be supplied at an extra charge.

Overall dimensions: Length, 11' 4". Width, 4' 9". Height, 5' 3".

EQUIPMENT.

Spare Wheel Carrier, Speedometer, Clock, Dash-Lamp, Petrol Gauge, Automatic Screen Wiper, 12-volt Electric Starter and 12-volt Lighting Set with Five Lamps, Centrally Grouped Instrument Board, Electric Horn, Licence Holder, Plain Number Plates and Full Kit of Tools and Spares.

Underslung worm of high efficiency in oil bath.

The 9 h.p. 'FALMOUTH' Fabric Saloon

The 9 h.p.
'FALMOUTH' Fabric Saloon

SPECIFICATION.

Body framed in ash, panelled where necessary, ensuring lightness and rigidity, external covering in two colours. Seats four full-sized adults. The front seats are adjustable. Four doors of ample width, each fitted with wind-up window. Three of the doors are provided with an inner locking device, the other can be locked from the outside. The upholstery is carried out in best quality moquette. Single panel sloping windscreen having central adjustment. Large rear light fitted with blind. Adequate mudguarding. Complete with five wheels and tyres. Choice of three colours—Red, Brown, Blue.

£215

Wire Wheels, **£10** extra.
Triplex glass can be supplied at an extra charge.

Overall dimensions : Length, 11' 4". Grid down, 12' 1½".
Width, 4' 9". Height, 5' 9". Approximate weight, 15 cwt.
Fitted with "Stanlite" folding head or sliding roof at the same price.

EQUIPMENT.

Luggage Grid, Driving Mirror, Speedometer, Clock, Dash-Lamp, Petrol Gauge, Automatic Screen Wiper, 12-volt Electric Starter and 12-volt Lighting Set with Five Lamps, Centrally Grouped Illuminated Instrument Board, Interior Light, Electric Horn, Licence Holder, Plain Number Plates and Full Kit of Tools and Spares.

"Stanlite" Folding Head giving open or closed car conditions. Specially suitable for people who want plenty of fresh air.

Upholstered in Leatherette.

"Stanlite" Sliding Roof. A 'Standard' development now perfected ; can be opened or closed at will even when the car is in motion. The 'Standard' car is the only popular priced car on which this refinement is available.

Upholstered in Repp.

The New "Standard"

All British

12/24 Horse Power Car

THE 12/24 H.P. "WELLESBOURNE"
5-Seater

SPECIFICATION

BODY.—Built of best ash framing, fitted with four doors, all of which have slam locks with inside and outside handles and door bumpers.

FRONT SEATS.—'Standard' patent independent adjustable bucket seats with folding back rests and provision for tools under the seat cushions and also in the toeboard locker.

PAINTWORK.—Highly finished in 'Standard' blue, crimson, or fawn to choice. Wheels, wings and bootings are painted black, and all bright parts are heavily nickel plated.

TRIMMING.—Body is trimmed in antique leather to match paintwork. The lower portion of the door is upholstered with a suitable hair carpet, pockets are provided in each door. A fibre mat is fitted in the front and a hair carpet in the rear compartment.

HOOD.—Patent "All-weather" hood, covered with black waterproof material.

SIDE WINDOWS.—'Standard' patent, made up on rigid frames, signalling flap fitted to front offside curtain. Curtains attached to the Body by dropping into two bushes on top of the doors. An arrangement enables a curtain to be partly opened for ventilation. All curtains open and close with each door and can remain up and used as side screens when the hood is folded down. When not in use, they are carried behind the rear cushion. A detachable quarter light is fitted.

WINDSCREEN.—Sloping adjustable type with swing top half. An automatic windscreen wiper is provided.

SCUTTLE DASH.—Combines instrument board and tray for parcels, etc. Finished in natural walnut. The dash ventilator is fitted and controlled from the instrument board.

APPROXIMATE OVERALL DIMENSIONS.—Length 12' 9". Width 5' 10". Height 6' 0".

TYRES.—Dunlop L.P. 28" × 4·95".

EQUIPMENT.—Spare Wheel and Tyre, Luggage Grid, Driving Mirror, Speedometer, Clock, Dash Lamp, Ash Tray, Electric Starter and Lighting Set with five lamps, Electric Horn, Hood Envelope, Petrol Can and Holder, Licence Holder, Spring Gaiters, Plain Number Plates. Full kit of Tools and Spares as on back page.

PRICE.—£275

THE 12/24 H.P. "PARK LANE"
Saloon

SPECIFICATION

BODY.—Built of best ash framing fitted with four doors, each having slam locks, door bumpers and flush inside lever. Panelled in specially prepared steel.

FRONT SEATS.—'Standard' patent independent adjustable bucket seats with folding back rests and provision for tools under the seat cushions and also in the toeboard locker.

PAINTWORK.—Highly finished in 'Standard' blue, crimson or fawn to choice. Wheels, wings and bootings are painted black, and all bright parts are heavily nickel plated.

TRIMMING.—Body trimmed in suitable Bedford Cord with cloth and laces for roof and quarters to match. The roof is partly panelled, and the remainder covered in black waterproof material, finished round the edge with special water channel. Rope pulls are fitted in the rear compartment. A fibre mat is fitted in the front and a pile carpet in the rear compartment.

WINDSCREEN.—Double type slightly sloping, top half swinging outwards, fitted with automatic screen wiper.

SCUTTLE DASH.—Combines instrument board and tray for parcels, etc. Finished in natural walnut. A dash ventilator is fitted and controlled from the instrument board.

APPROXIMATE OVERALL DIMENSIONS.—Length 12' 9". Width 5 10". Height 5' 11".

TYRES.—Dunlop L.P. 28" × 4·95".

EQUIPMENT.—Spare Wheel and Tyre, Luggage Grid, Driving Mirror, Speedometer, Clock, Dash Lamp, Ash Tray, Ladies' and Gents' Companion, Electric Starter and Lighting Set with five lamps, Electric Horn, Roof Net, Roof Lamp, Roof Ventilator, Petrol Can and Carrier, Licence Holder, Spring Gaiters, Number Plates. Full kit of Spares as on back page.

PRICE.—£335

THE 12/24 H.P. CHASSIS

SPECIFICATION

ENGINE.—Four Cylinder, 75 m/m bore × 110 m/m stroke. (c.c. 1944).

CYLINDERS.—Cast *en bloc*, three bearing crankshaft, "H" section Duralumin connecting rods and aluminium pistons. Cylinder head detachable.

VALVES.—Mushroom type, overhead, operated by Push rods and rockers, all in line, rocker shaft being force lubricated from main supply.

LUBRICATION.—Forced feed by means of pump, oil being forced through the camshaft and crankshaft bearings and through the drilled crank to the connecting rod bearings, valve rocker shaft force lubricated.

IGNITION.—Magneto.

STARTING AND LIGHTING.—Electric.

PETROL SUPPLY.—Gravity, tank in Dash.

COOLING.—Thermo-syphon, large capacity Radiator of gilled tube type assisted by fan.

CLUTCH.—Double disc, metal driving plates engaging with flywheel, centre plate and clutch cover. Clutch is enclosed.

GEARBOX.—Three speeds forward and reverse, operated by right hand gate change, gears are manufactured throughout from finest alloy steel.

GEAR RATIOS.—Top, 4·6 ; 2nd, 8·05 ; 1st, 18·4.

PROPELLER SHAFT.—Open Propeller shaft, fabric joints

BRAKES.—Footbrake of expanding type operating on large steel drums on all four wheels. Handbrake of contracting type operating on drum on rear end of gearshaft. All brakes bonded asbestos lined, liners being renewable.

REAR AXLE.—Of substantial design mounted on ball bearings throughout. Worm gear of the overhead type.

FRONT AXLE.—"H" section, Nickel Steel stamping of substantial dimensions stiffened at outer ends to take the torque of frontwheel brakes.

SHOCK ABSORBERS.—Fitted to front and rear axles.

WHEELS.—Steel detachable, black enamelled.

TYRES.—Dunlop L.P. 28″ × 4·95″.

WHEELBASE.—9′ 4″. **TRACK.**—4′ 8″. **GROUND CLEARANCE.**—9½″.

CHASSIS PRICE.—£215

TOOLS.		SPARE PARTS,	
1 Tool Box.	1 Oil Can.	1 Valve Spring.	1 Valve Collar.
1 Open Ended Spanner, ⅜″ × ½″.	1 Petrol Funnel.	1 Pair Brake Springs—Rear Wheel Brake.	1 Valve Cotter.
1 Open Ended Spanner, ⁹⁄₁₆″ × ⅝″.	1 Sponge Cloth.		1 Gauge for Valve Clearance.
1 Open Ended Spanner, ⁷⁄₁₆″ × ½″.	1 Carburetter Key.	1 Exhaust Pipe Packing.	
1 Adjustable Spanner.	1 Cold Chisel.	1 Top Water Pipe Joint.	4 Adjusting Plates Rear Wheel Brake.
1 Double Ended Spanner.	1 File.	1 Hallite Jointing 6″ sq.	
1 Tube Spanner, ⅝″ × ⅝″.	2 Pin Punches (⅛″ & ¼″).	1 Soft Steel Wire, 6′.	1 Valve Rocker Ball Pin.
1 Tube Spanner for Gear Striker Screw and Oil Base Nuts.	1 Combustion Chamber Cleaner.	12 Assorted Nuts.	
		12 Assorted Plain Washers.	
1 ¼″ Tommy Bar (Taper).	1 Pump.	12 Assorted Spring Washers.	1 Carburetter Handbook
1 ¼″ Tommy Bar.	1 Detachable Wheel Brace.	12 Assorted C. & A. Washers.	1 Magneto Handbook.
1 Magneto Spanner.	1 Rear Hub Remover and Screw.	1 Box Assorted Split Pins.	1 'Standard' Instruction Book.
1 Hammer.		1 Grease Gun complete.	
1 Pair Pliers.	1 Jack and Handle.	1 Grease Nipple, ⅛″ gas.	
Combination Tool for Recess and Saw Cut Screws.			

COUNT THEM ON THE ROAD

THE STANDARD MOTOR COMPANY, LTD., COVENTRY.

London Showrooms : 49, Pall Mall, S.W.1

W. W. CURTIS, LTD., COVENTRY.

The top picture shows a Standard car racing at Brooklands during the late 'twenties, whilst below is a four-door fabric-bodied saloon from 1928.

"NOW do you believe me?"

Some people wonder how a saloon with the luxurious comfort of the Standard "Pall Mall" can be made for £435, and when they have taken a trial run in one they wonder still more.

The 18-36 h.p. 6-cyl. Standard "Pall Mall" Saloon sacrifices nothing to price, in either quality or performance. It is fast; with five up it climbs without effort; it is easy to control and look after; it is very comfortable and roomy. Inside and out, it looks like a £600 car. Yet it is only £435 complete. Write to-day for full information and an appointment for a free trial.

"Count them on the Road."

The All British
Standard

18-36 h.p. 6 Cyl. "Pall Mall" Saloon

18-36 h.p. 6-Cylinder
"Stratford" Tourer
£315
Dunlop Tyres

£435

All Standard Cars are finished in the Zofelac Cellulose Process. Colours: Red, Blue and Fawn.

The Standard Motor Co., Ltd., Coventry.
London Showrooms: 49, Pall Mall, SW1.

Agents everywhere.

"THE AUTOCAR" ROAD TESTS

9 h.p. STANDARD SPORTS SALOON.

THERE is no question but that the car with a relatively small engine is becoming more and more popular, and that the owner wants as much power as he can obtain provided that the engine is not unduly harsh and that it remains reliable.

The 9 h.p. Standard sports model recently tested is an interesting machine because it was fitted with the latest type Gordon England fabric saloon ; it happened to be tested in the very middle of a heat wave—at the worst possible time for a saloon body.

Now, the most interesting point about the little car was that it was cooler than one would have imagined to be possible in such circumstances. The ventilation consists of a perforated tube running along the top of the windscreen, a skylight opening at the back, and two front windows, of which the panels slide over one another, forming an air gap forward and astern. The result seems to be a continuous current of fresh air running along under the roof, and the occupants do not suffer from the baked feeling that is one of the drawbacks of some saloons in hot weather.

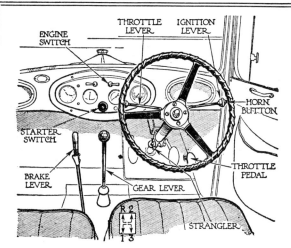

DATA FOR THE DRIVER.

Engine : 9 h.p. four cylinders, 60 × 102 mm. (1,153 c.c.).
Tax £9.
Wheelbase 7ft. 8in., track 3ft. 9in.
Overall length 12ft. 1⅛in., width 4ft. 9in., height 5ft. 6in.
Tyres 27 × 4.4in. on detachable steel wheels.

Engine—rear-axle gear ratios	Maxima (m.p.h.)	Acceleration (10–30 m.p.h.)
20 to 1	17	—
9.8 to 1	33	6¼ secs.
5 to 1	51	15 secs.

Turning circle 36ft.
Tank capacity 6 gallons, fuel consumption 40 m.p.g.
Weight of complete car 14 cwt. 2 qr. 2 lb.
Weight per c.c. 1.3 lb.
Twelve-volt lighting set cuts in at 15 m.p.h., 7 amps at 20 m.p.h.
Price £245.

21 FEET from 25 M.P.H.

Brake test from 25. m.p.h.

Externally the body looks well, particularly with the new fabric-covered bonnet, which makes the car rather less stubby. There is a reasonable amount of room in the rear seats, the pneumatic upholstery is comfortable, while the body generally is fitted out rather in the manner of expensive and luxurious town carriages intended for much larger chassis. The fact that there are only two doors is not so much a handicap as one might anticipate, because the doors are very wide and the front seats tilt.

On the instrument board, on either side of the grouped instruments, are two cubby holes useful for gloves or pipes or maps, but these would be better if so constructed that articles stowed in them did not fall out when the car is moving, as is the tendency at present. Some of the glass was a little wavy, though it could not be said that this seriously interfered with the view.

Luggage can be accommodated in a proper fabric-covered suit-case container which forms part of the body at the back, and there are also two useful cupboards

"The Autocar" Road Tests.

that serve also as arm-rests for the passengers in the rear seats.

The engine of this particular car had, it was understood, been altered slightly for a competition, the compression of the engine having been raised rather more than standard, with the result that it was on the harsh side. The performance can be judged from the table given on the previous page, the acceleration on second gear being extraordinarily good.

With four passengers the car is considerably more comfortable than with two, owing to there being a slightly choppy action of the springs, possibly due to the short wheelbase (as noticeable with other small cars of about the same size). This is really only experienced on abnormally bad roads, and is damped out by extra load.

The steering is easy to handle, but might perhaps have a trifle of additional castor angle. The brakes are very good, and the only point that really needs watching is the clutch, which, owing to the very slight movement, is liable to be very fierce until the driver becomes thoroughly accustomed to the machine.

Generally speaking, the little car would be ideal for town work, because it is very easy to handle, economical to run, and not large enough to be awkward in car parks or in traffic.

A 1930 Avon Special based on the Standard "Nine" chassis.

MORE NEW CARS
STANDARD CARS FOR 1930

FOLLOWING the declared policy of the Standard Company, no changes in definite types are being made for next year, and production will be concentrated upon the 9 h.p. four-cylinder and the 15 h.p. six-cylinder cars. All new cars which leave the works after the present date will be 1930 models, and the prices will be stabilised. For those who require more body space on the 15 h.p. chassis this will also be produced with a cylinder bore increased to 65.5 mm. Known as the Envoy, this model has a very shapely body, an improved radiator, and other special points which will be mentioned later.

Of the range of 9 h.p. four-cylinder cars the least expensive is the Fulham, a four-door four-light saloon, of which the price remains unaltered at £185. The car, however, will be available in black as well as in a brown finish and with a waistline of any colour. A sliding roof can be provided at an extra charge of £5.

No alteration has been made in the

Concentration on the 9 h.p. Four-cylinder and 15 h.p. Six-cylinder Types. Additional 15 h.p. Model with Longer Wheelbase.

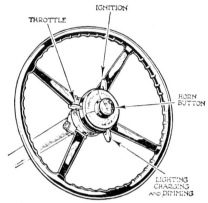

An up-to-date and sensible control box in the centre of the Standard Envoy steering wheel.

also the gear lever has been lengthened so that it comes conveniently to the left hand.

Last year there was a Teignmouth Special model which cost £245. Its extra equipment included safety glass, wire wheels of special colours, companions, dipping lamps, roof net, head cushions, and a choice of either leather upholstery or chromium plating. If it had the two last-mentioned features this model was called the Imperial and was priced at £255. In future, all the fittings mentioned will be included in a car to be termed the Teignmouth Special and offered at £250.

Introduced as it was only a month or two ago, and remarkable for the comfort in the bodywork as well as for the arrangement of the boot to take suit-cases of normal sizes, the 9 h.p. coupé will be continued at the original figure of £250, but the body has four instead of two lights and the improved type of bucket seats.

9 h.p. Teignmouth coach-built saloon.

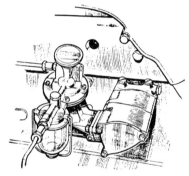

In place of a vacuum tank a petrol pump driven from the engine provides the fuel feed on the 15 h.p. six-cylinder Standard Envoy model.

price of that increasingly popular type, the 9 h.p. Teignmouth saloon, and it remains at £215. The body, which has a sliding roof, is now covered with a fine grain fabric, and has chromium-plated exterior fittings. The range of colours has been increased, and to black and to blue finishes an attractive shade of grey has been added. The cars will be obtainable in any one of these colours or in combinations of any two.

Another considerable improvement in the appearance is that the interior colour schemes are now arranged to harmonise with the exterior shade. Increased comfort is secured by front seats two inches higher in the back and two inches longer in the cushion ;

9 h.p. Teignmouth Special with six lights.

STANDARD CARS FOR 1930—*(continued).*

Improved 9 h.p. Standard Selby tourer.

Then there is a 9 h.p. coachbuilt saloon with six lights, finished in dual brown colour or dual blue, priced at £235, the specification being identical with that of the Teignmouth. In future there will be no open two-seater touring model, but the Selby four-seater touring body has been revised and improved in appearance and the price raised to £195; this sum, it should be emphasised, includes leather upholstery and chromium plating, in addition to a dual finish.

In the range of 15 h.p. six-cylinder cars the Exmouth six-light, fabric-covered saloon, with sliding roof, a very popular model, will be unaltered, and the price remains at £325. Also the Tourist coupé, with a four-light body, remains unchanged at £365.

Next comes the Envoy model already referred to, with the longer wheelbase, spiral-bevel final drive, petrol pump in place of a vacuum tank, front dumb-irons closed in with a shield, silentbloc spring bushes, and

a larger six-light four-door body with a sliding roof. This is available at £340. There is also an Envoy Special offered at £365, with the additional equipment of safety glass, coloured wire wheels, one-shot lubrication, chromium plating, companions, head cushions, roof nets, and other details.

Special features of the Envoy model include a longer gear lever working in a concealed gate and having a spring reverse stop instead of a catch. Alterations have been made to the steering and the steering box is now carried on the frame to reduce vibration, whilst at the centre of the steering wheel is an extremely neat circular control box with levers for ignition and throttle, a central button for the horn, a control for the dipping reflector headlamp system, and switches for the lamps. This is an up-to-date and very well-carried-out fitting.

It will be realised that there are some very attractive cars indeed in the Standard range for next year.

The 15 h.p. six-cylinder Standard Envoy, which has a longer wheelbase, a larger body and a larger engine than the earlier model.

AN AMERICAN F.W.D. CAR

IT is extremely interesting to find a big American manufacturer putting into production a car with front-wheel drive, because in America this form of drive has been developed chiefly for use on racing cars at Indianapolis. The controversy, too, as to the possibilities of this method of propulsion in racing has just reached its height.

The new machine is termed the Cord and is built by the firm responsible for the construction of the Auburn. The engine is a Lycoming rated at 33.8 h.p., having a bore of 82.55 mm. and a stroke of 114.3 mm.—having a capacity, that is, of nearly five litres. The bell-housing for the clutch is, of course, on the nose of the crank case, and the drive passes straight forward to the

gear box. With the last-mentioned component is incorporated a bevel final drive in a casing, on either side of which are the brake shoes for the front wheel

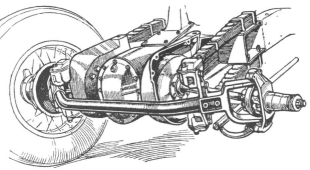

Front axle of the eight-cylinder F.W.D. Cord.

brakes. The driving shafts are provided with two universal joints, of which one is at the centre of the front wheel, between the forks of the axle end, the wheel spindle being attached to the fork and there being no pivot pin as such.

The frame is straight and is stiffened amidships by a gigantic X-shaped girder, while the front wheels are each sprung on two quarter-elliptic leaf springs, one clipped to the top, the other to the bottom of the frame. The rear wheels are carried on an H-section axle with half-elliptic springs and big hydraulic shock absorbers, and, naturally, each wheel runs independently on the axle. There is a front axle, which is unusual for a front-wheel-drive car, the axle

"THE AUTOCAR" ROAD TESTS

15 h.p. STANDARD ENVOY SALOON.

INTRODUCED specifically to cater for those who want a roomy car which is not heavy and is economical to own and run, the Envoy model of the six-cylinder Standard has only recently been added to the range. As compared with the normal Standard Six, the 15 h.p. type, this new edition has an engine with a slightly larger bore, 65.5 mm. as against 63.5 mm., and a capacity of 2,054 c.c. instead of one of 1,930 c.c. As the wheelbase of the Envoy type is seven inches longer, and the track is two inches wider, so as to accommodate a larger body, the actual performance of the car produces much the same figures. But there is a considerable difference in the manner of the performance, indeed a marked improvement.

One of the features of the Envoy is the enhanced smoothness of the engine. The steering box is mounted on the frame instead of on the engine and gear box unit, with the result that engine vibration is not communicated to the hands of the driver. Also the steering itself is more free from road snatch, and affords a pleasant compromise between lightness, caster action, and a not too low ratio. It is perhaps a shade on the "vague" side until the driver becomes accustomed to it, but the car is certainly not in the least tiring to drive.

Another point where im-

Longer Wheelbase Model with Slightly Larger Engine Gives a Decidedly Improved Performance.

There is easy access to the saloon body.

provement is to be noted is in the gear change, which has a long lever coming comfortably to the hand, and is not so tricky to master as the earlier type could be. Also the performance on third gear is good, better than it was, and early changes at 40 m.p.h. can be essayed when a stiff climb is started.

The single-plate clutch is of an improved type and takes up the drive smoothly when the car is starting from rest, sufficiently so to pass the test of starting actually on top gear. With normal loads over normal roads the car is very much the mount for a lazy driver, who starts in second gear, changes straight into top gear, and stays there for most of the run. The flexibility on top gear is good; it is possible to take most ordinary slopes on this ratio, and to crawl along in traffic on it. Incidentally, the Envoy model has a Solex carburetter. There is no cover plate over the top of the engine, as on the other Six, and the feed to the carburetter is by means of an excellent mechanical petrol pump driven from the camshaft. Battery ignition is used.

On hills of the steeper variety the car renders a good account of itself. Gradients of 1 in 10 can be climbed on top at speeds varying according to the straightness or curvature of the road, and without need of rushing.

" THE AUTOCAR " ROAD TESTS—*(continued).*

Hills of 1 in 6½ need third speed, and are surmounted at speeds between 16 and 20 m.p.h. Second gear will deal with almost any kind of severe main-road hill, and first will take the car with a full load up almost anything that can be called a road, and on which the driving wheels will grip.

One of the special features is the way in which the car holds the road. It corners fast and with perfect steadiness, and on slippery surfaces it is disinclined to skid. The suspension is fair with a light load and good with a full complement. The brakes are powerful and also smooth, and they do not require frequent adjustment. In wet weather the front brakes are inclined to grow fierce, but this is easily avoided if the driver occasionally applies the brakes lightly to keep them sweet. In very hilly country these brakes give the driver much confidence.

Plenty of Room.

In the body there is really sufficient room for five full-sized persons, and their heads are well clear of the roof. Separate and immediately adjustable bucket seats are provided in front, and they have backs high enough to give proper support under the shoulders. Beneath the front-seat cushions are the batteries, which can be reached in a few seconds for topping up. The tools are carried in a locker underneath the bonnet.

A word of special praise is due to the sliding roof. It works admirably, and does not allow a single drop of water to enter even in a storm. It is typical of all the coachwork—simply and plainly carried out, but very efficient, and not prone to

15 h.p. STANDARD ENVOY SALOON.

VC·1690

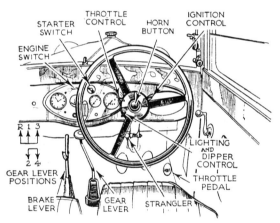

STARTER SWITCH — THROTTLE CONTROL — HORN BUTTON — IGNITION CONTROL — ENGINE SWITCH — R 1 3 / 2 4 GEAR LEVER POSITIONS — BRAKE LEVER — GEAR LEVER — STRANGLER — LIGHTING AND DIPPER CONTROL — THROTTLE PEDAL

DATA FOR THE DRIVER.

16 h.p., six cylinders, 65.5 × 102mm. (2,054 c.c.).
Tax £16.
Wheelbase 9ft. 10in., track 4ft. 8in.
Overall length 13ft. 9in., width 5ft. 8in., height 6ft. 0in.
Tyres 29 × 5in. on detachable steel wheels.

Engine—rear axle gear ratios.	Maxima (m.p.h.).	Acceleration (10–30 m.p.h.).
20	20	—
11.6	34	8 sec.
8·35	46	9 sec.
5.2	58	13 sec.

Turning circle : 42ft.
Tank capacity 10½ gallons, fuel consumption 24 m.p.g.
12-volt lighting set, two-rate charging.
Weight : 25 cwt.
Price, with fabric saloon body, £340.

24 FEET FROM 25 M·P·H

develop annoying and elusive rattles or squeaks.

The wings, too, are stoutly attached, and their shape, with deep valances on the outer edges, is effective in keeping the car clean. There is not a great deal of work to be done as regards maintenance. A single grease-gun nipple supplies practically all the chassis bearings, there being only eight other nipples to require attention. Silent-bloc bushes for the spring eyes and shackles obviate the necessity of any lubrication at these points.

Handy Controls.

The controls are very well arranged. In the centre of the steering wheel is a circular box from which three short levers protrude ; the upper pair attend respectively to ignition and to throttle setting, whilst the lower lever is a switch for altering the charging rate, and for the side and tail lamps, the head lamps, and the head lamp " dip and switch " movement. The head lamps are the excellent Lucas Biflex and the dipping reflector is electrically operated instead of pneumatically, as on the other Standard Six.

The horn button is in the centre of the control box, and the horn responds instantaneously. The car's specification includes many worth-while details, such as chromium plating, leather upholstery, driving mirror and blind, concealed illumination for the instrument board, valance over the front dumb irons, strong luggage grid, and so forth.

Taking it all the way round the Standard Envoy is a remarkable car for the money, and one that functions well in every respect, whilst the body in particular is spacious and very roomy.

RESPONSIBILITY

RESPONSIBILITY can be either a handicap or an encouragement.

For those who lack courage or initiative it is a burden.

For others—the strong and progressive—it is an urge to succeed. Its presence demands care and forethought, increased effort and patience. Its ready acceptance creates confidence in those who bear it.

The Standard Motor Company recognise their responsibility and accept it gladly. Every effort is made to maintain and improve the high reputation for Quality and Value that has been earned by Standard cars.

A defect in detail will mar any vehicle—may even have serious consequences.

The name of Standard is a Hall Mark of Quality—it has earned the confidence of both Trade and public —it guarantees you the best car in its class.

All-British Standard

PASSENGER AIR LINERS
Modern civilization demands the ready acceptance of responsibility. The Air Liner pilot—quick in emergency—is an outstanding example.

Models for 1931

"ENVOY"	"ENSIGN" SIX	"BIG NINE"
Six-Cylinder Half-Panelled Saloon	Six Cylinder Saloons—as illustrated	Four Cylinder Saloons
£385	£245 £275 £285	From £195—£255

'Dunlop Tyres as Standard

THE STANDARD MOTOR COMPANY LTD COVENTRY

NOTES AND NEWS.

*Miss Paddy Naismith with her Standard
"Little Nine" Avon Coupe.*

STANDARD AVON SUCCESSES.

MISS Paddy Naismith, driving a Standard 'Little Nine' Avon Coupe competed in the recent Ulster Rally and Concours d'Elegance with gratifying success.

She drove from Dover to Heysham, and there were several checks on this part of the journey, but not secret ones. Then she crossed by boat to Belfast and the last part of the journey to Bangor in Northern Ireland was a very severe one as regards secret checks, the maximum allowance being 30 secs., either way. It seems she lost the £100 prize by being 41 seconds out at one of these checks and consequently lost three marks. She did, however, win the Ladies' Cup in her Class. Next day she paraded in the Concours d'Elegance, having polished up the car, and won first prize in the 10 h.p. class. Both these efforts reflect considerable credit on the Standard Motor Company and the New Avon Body Co., as the one illuminates the regular running of the chassis, and the other the good looks of the body.

Following upon these achievements comes news of the success of a Standard Avon 'Sixteen' owned by Mr. J. Salem of Manchester, who was awarded Grand Prix d'Honneur in the Concours d'Elegance recently held at La Baule, France.

*Mr. J. Salem with his Standard Avon Swan
"Sixteen" which won first prize in the recent
Concours d' Elegance, La Baule, France.*

AVON COUPE—SIX CYLINDER SIXTEEN CHASSIS

AVON COUPE—"LITTLE-9" CHASSIS

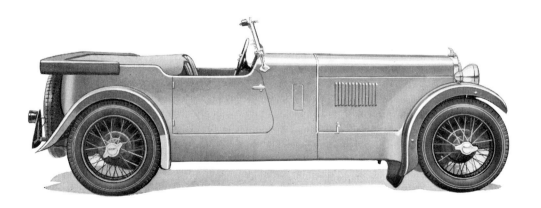

THE AVON SPECIAL FOUR-SEATER TOURER.

By THE NEW AVON BODY CO., LTD.,
WARWICK.

AVON CLOSE-COUPLED COUPE—6-CYLINDER SIXTEEN CHASSIS.

AVON OPEN SPORTS—"LITTLE-9" CHASSIS

AVON COUPE—"BIG-9" CHASSIS

By THE NEW AVON BODY CO. LTD.,
WARWICK.

STANDARD MODELS FOR 1932

A new Two-Seater Tourer on the Standard "Little Nine," "Big Nine" and "Sixteen" Chassis

The Two-Seater Tourer on the 1932 "Big Nine" Standard chassis

The body of this neat and exceptionally roomy touring model is coachbuilt and metal panelled, with two wide doors. Finished in cellulose, and upholstered in finest quality leather, it is available in the following attractive colour schemes: *Blue with blue leather, Maroon with red leather, Condor Grey with brown leather, Black with either red, brown or green leather.* Black wire wheels. The hood, which is covered with best quality twill with envelope to match, can be supplied in colours to harmonise with colour of car.

Incorporated in the construction of this model is a cunningly concealed and very roomy two-seater dickey seat. Behind the two front seats, which are of the semi-bucket type (instantly and independently adjustable) is a space which provides a most convenient storage place for suit cases or other light luggage which is not only accessible but protected from the weather when the hood is up.

The special adjustable windscreen is fitted with Protectoglass, the celluloid side screens with adjustable opening signalling traps. The side screens are easily removable and can be stored behind dickey seat squab.

"Little Nine"	£145	Ex-Works
"Big Nine"	£195	Ex-Works
"Sixteen"	£225	Ex-Works

the STANDARD
by which all other cars are judged

THE 1932 STANDARD "LITTLE NINE"

ENGINE. 4-cylinder. 60.25 m.m. bore × 88 m.m. stroke. 1005 c.c. Tax £9. Side valves. Lubrication by gear pump. Petrol supply from 5-gallon tank at rear of chassis. Autovac feed. Ignition battery and coil. 6-volt lighting set. Head lamp dimming device. GEARBOX: Three speed, silent second. Central control. REAR AXLE: Spiral bevel. STEERING: Worm and nut, very light in operation. SPRINGS: Half-elliptic, friction type shock absorbers front and rear. Wire wheels, 27″ × 4″. Dunlop tyres. Spare wheel and tyre carried at rear. BRAKES: Bendix Duo Servo operating on all four wheels.
DIMENSIONS: Wheelbase, 7′ 6″. Track, 3′ 8″. Length, 10′ 11″. Width, 4′ 5″. Equipment includes luggage grid, driving mirror, speedometer, clock, oil pressure gauge, automatic screen wiper, electric horn, licence holder, full kit of tools.

THE 1932 STANDARD "BIG NINE"

ENGINE. 4-cylinder, 63.5 m.m. bore × 102 m.m. stroke. 1287 c.c. Tax £10. Side valves, pump lubrication. Petrol supply from 9-gallon tank at rear of chassis. Electric gauge on dash. Ignition battery and coil. 12-volt lighting and starting set. Five lamps and rear stop lamp. Dip and switch head lamps controlled from above steering wheel. GEARBOX: Four-speed, silent third. STEERING: Marles Weller. SPRINGS: Half-elliptic. Luvax Hydraulic shock absorbers front and rear. Wire wheels, 27″ × 4.4″. Dunlop tyres. Spare wheel carried at rear. BRAKES: Bendix Duo Servo on all four wheels.
DIMENSIONS: Wheelbase, 8′ 4¼″. Track, 4′ 0″. Length, 12′ 0″. Width, 5′ 1″. Equipment includes luggage grid, driving mirror, electric screen wiper, electric clock, horn, full kit of tools. Licence holder.

THE 1932 STANDARD "SIXTEEN"

ENGINE. 6-cylinder. 65.5 m.m. bore × 101.6 m.m. stroke. 2054 c.c. Tax £16. Side valves. Gear type pump lubrication. Seven bearing crankshaft. Petrol supply from 9-gallon tank at rear of chassis. Petrol pump feed. Ignition, battery and coil. 12-volt lighting and starting set. Five lamps and rear stop lamp. Head lamps dip and switch control on steering wheel. GEARBOX: Four-speed, silent third. REAR AXLE. Spiral bevel. STEERING: Marles Weller. SPRINGS: Half-elliptic. Luvax shock absorbers front and rear. BRAKES: Bendix Duo Servo on all four wheels. Wire wheels, 29″ × 5″. Dunlop tyres. Spare wheel at rear. DIMENSIONS: Wheelbase, 9′ 1″. Track, 4′ 0″. Length, 13′ 0″. Width, 5′ 1″. EQUIPMENT: As given for "Big Nine."

Note:—For further details than the above regarding chassis and equipment see specifications of Saloon models of same type in the Standard 1932 catalogue.

THE STANDARD MOTOR COMPANY LIMITED
CANLEY   COVENTRY

THE STANDARD 'LITTLE NINE'

COACHBUILT SALOON, in attractive choice of colours, moulding and finest quality leather cloth pleated style upholstery to harmonise, head cloth and carpets to match (*See chart inside back cover*). Four wide doors, fitted with wind-up windows, and all doors provided with convenient locking device. Front seats are semi-bucket type, instantly and independently adjustable. Provision is made in all doors for the carrying of maps and similar articles, and there are two recesses in dash for small parcels.

Complete with five wire wheels and Dunlop tyres, adjustable

Protectoglass screen, pile carpet, rear window blind, rear vision mirror, luggage grid, shock absorbers, screen wiper, speedometer, clock, oil pressure gauge, electric horn, licence holder and full kit of tools. Exterior bright fittings, except lamps, chromium plated.

SPECIAL COACHBUILT SALOON, with specification as above, but including the following extra equipment : Furniture hide upholstery, Protectoglass all round, ash tray, cigar lighter, hat cord, rope pulls, chromium plated lamps, bumper bars front and rear, interior roof light.

FOR PRICES SEE INSIDE COVER

THE STANDARD 'BIG NINE'

COACHBUILT SALOON, in attractive choice of colours, moulding and finest quality leather cloth pleated style upholstery to harmonise, head cloth and carpets to match (*See chart inside back cover*). Four wide doors, fitted with wind-up windows, and all doors provided with convenient locking device. Front seats are semi-bucket type, instantly and independently adjustable. Provision is made in all doors for the carrying of maps and similar articles, two recesses in dash for small parcels. Arm rests are fitted to rear seats.

Complete with five wire wheels and Dunlop tyres, adjustable

Protectoglass screen, pile carpet, rear window blind, rear vision mirror, luggage grid, shock absorbers, speedometer, clock, petrol gauge on dash, oil pressure gauge, interior light, electric horn, electric screen wiper, licence holder, and full kit of tools. Exterior bright fittings, except lamps, chromium plated. Rear stop light.

SPECIAL COACHBUILT SALOON, with specification as above, but including the following extra equipment : Furniture hide upholstery, Protectoglass all round, ash tray, cigar lighter, hat cord, chromium plated lamps, bumper bars front and rear.

FOR PRICES SEE INSIDE COVER

THE STANDARD 'SIXTEEN'

COACHBUILT SALOON, in attractive choice of colours, moulding and finest quality leather cloth pleated style upholstery to harmonise, head cloth and carpets to match (*See chart inside back cover*). Four wide doors, fitted with wind-up windows, and all doors provided with convenient locking device. Front seats are semi-bucket type, instantly and independently adjustable. Provision is made in all doors for the carrying of maps and similar light articles, two recesses in dash for small parcels. Arm rests are fitted to rear seats. Complete with five wire wheels and Dunlop tyres, adjustable Protectoglass screen, pile carpet, rear

window blind, rear vision mirror, luggage grid, shock absorbers, speedometer, electric clock, petrol gauge on dash, oil pressure gauge, interior light, electric horn, electric screen wiper, licence holder and full kit of tools. Exterior bright fittings, except lamps, chromium plated. Rear stop light.

SPECIAL COACHBUILT SALOON, with specification as above, but including the following extra equipment : Furniture hide upholstery, Protectoglass all round, ash tray, cigar lighter, hat cord, chromium plated lamps, bumper bars front and rear.

FOR PRICES SEE INSIDE COVER

THE STANDARD 'TWENTY'

COACHBUILT SALOON, in attractive choice of colours, moulding and finest quality furniture hide pleated style upholstery to harmonise, head cloths and carpets to match (*See chart inside back cover*). Four wide doors, fitted with wind-up windows, all doors provided with convenient locking device. The seating accommodation is generous both front and rear. Front seats are instantly and independently adjustable, and have folding tables concealed in the back. Arm rests are fitted to rear seat. Pockets are fitted to all doors, two recesses in dash for light articles.

Complete with five wire wheels and Dunlop tyres, adjustable Protectoglass screen, pile carpet, rear window blind, rear vision

mirror, luggage grid, shock absorbers, speedometer, electric clock, electric petrol guage on dash, oil pressure gauge, interior light, electric horn, electric screen wiper, licence holder, and full kit of tools. Exterior bright fittings, except lamps, chromium plated. Rear stop light. (*Option of 16 or 20 h.p. engine*).

SPECIAL COACHBUILT SALOON, with specification as above, but including the following extra equipment : Protectoglass all round, bumper bars, chromium plated lamps, ash tray including cigar lighter, hat cord, specially luxurious front seats, folding centre arm rest in rear, additional spare wheel and Dunlop tyre.

FOR PRICES SEE INSIDE COVER

THE STANDARD FOUR-SEATER TOURER

This distinctive and graceful touring body, like all other Standard models, has an unusual amount of useful room for both driver and passengers. The body is coachbuilt with pressed steel panels and four wide doors, finished in cellulose and upholstered in finest quality leather in the following most attractive colour schemes : *Blue with blue leather, maroon with red leather, Condor grey with brown leather, black with either red, brown or green leather.* Black wire wheels.

Both hood and envelope can be supplied in colours to harmonise, the hood being covered in best quality twill with envelopes to match.

Front seats are semi-bucket type, instantly and independently adjustable. The special adjustable windscreen is fitted with Protectoglass, the celluloid side screens with adjustable opening signalling windows. Side screens are easily removed and stored behind rear squab. Doors are fitted with pockets and there are recesses in dash for light articles.

The Standard four-seater tourer is available on the "Little Nine," "Big Nine" and "Sixteen" Standard chassis. For full details regarding chassis and equipment see descriptions of Saloon models and also chassis specifications.

FOR PRICES SEE INSIDE COVER

THE STANDARD TWO-SEATER TOURER

The body of this neat and exceptionally roomy touring model is coachbuilt and metal panelled, with two wide doors. Finished in cellulose, and upholstered in finest quality leather, it is available in the following attractive colour schemes : *Blue with blue leather, maroon with red leather, Condor grey with brown leather, black with either red, brown or green leather.* Black wire wheels. The hood, which is covered with best quality twill with envelope to match, can be supplied in colours to harmonise with colour of car. Incorporated in the construction of this model is a cunningly concealed and very roomy two-seater dickey seat. Behind the two front seats, which are of the semi-bucket type (instantly and independently adjustable) is a space which provides a most convenient storage place for suit cases or other light luggage which is not only accessible but protected from the weather when the hood is up.

The special adjustable windscreen is fitted with Protectoglass, the celluloid side screens with adjustable opening signalling windows. The side screens are easily removable and can be stored behind dickey seat squab.

The Standard two-seater tourer is available on the "Little Nine," "Big Nine" and "Sixteen" Standard chassis. For full details regarding chassis and equipment see descriptions of Saloon models and also chassis specifications.

FOR PRICES SEE INSIDE COVER

THE STANDARD 'LITTLE NINE' DROP HEAD COUPÉ

Built to accommodate two large people in roomy comfort and to provide adequate and accessible provision for luggage, this extremely attractive drop head coupé body is fitted to the "Little Nine" chassis, details of which are given on page 18. The body is metal panelled, and provided with two exceptionally wide doors. The upholstery is attractively carried out in furniture hide in colours to harmonise with the exterior cellulose colour schemes (see chart). The seats are of the one piece type and are easily adjustable. The drop head is of simple and light design, and is very easily raised or lowered. It is covered in best quality cloth faced, rubber proofed black twill and provided with rear window. The side windows are of the wind-up type, and

can be operated both when head is up or down. Both the adjustable screen and the side windows are fitted with Protectoglass. The space behind the seats is for luggage and is accessible either from inside the body or by opening the lid of the boot from outside on which the spare wheel is carried. Doors are fitted with pockets, for maps, etc., and there are two recesses in dash for light articles. The centrally grouped instrument board is illuminated from behind panel. The equipment includes the following :—Bumper bars front and rear, chromium plated lamps, driving mirror, speedometer, clock, automatic screen wiper, electric horn, licence holder, complete tool kit.

FOR PRICES SEE INSIDE COVER

CLOSE-COUPLED HALF-PANELLED SALOON

Four-door four-light close-coupled Sports Saloon with flush fitting weather proof sliding roof, and large luggage container built flush with body sides, the lid of which carries the spare wheel and when fully opened acts as a luggage grid.

The body is completely panelled below the waistline, and covered with best quality black fabric above.

All the doors can be separately locked, three by means of safety catch on the lock and near-side front door with a private key. The front seats are of the adjustable bucket type and rear seat has ample accommodation for two passengers by making use of deep footwells.

Body throughout is fitted with safety glass, door glasses being raised or lowered by means of mechanical window regulators operated by handle.

Single panel windscreen made to open with adjustment for amount of opening required. Rear compartment is fitted with cigar lighter and ash tray.

A rear blind operated from driver's seat together with interior driving mirror, interior electric roof lamp, silk rope pulls and pockets incorporated in the trimming of all four doors. Cushions and squabs made up on Spring Cases, well stuffed and covered with best quality Celstra Hide.

FOR PRICES SEE INSIDE COVER

The chassis of the 1932 Standard "Little Nine" showing the extreme simplicity of layout. The fuel tank is at the rear.

THE STANDARD 'LITTLE NINE'

BRIEF CHASSIS SPECIFICATION.

ENGINE. Four cylinder. 60.25 m/m bore, 88 m/m stroke, 1005 c.c. Tax £9. Side valves. Exceptionally stiff crankshaft, two bearing type, both dynamically and statically balanced. Aluminium pistons, Duralumin connecting rods. Detachable cylinder head. Lubrication by gear type pump, supplying oil under pressure to main bearings of crankshaft, camshaft, and to big ends. All oil passages are drilled integral with cylinder block. A dip stick in the sump indicates quantity of oil, while pressure is recorded by gauge on dash. Ignition by coil and battery, automatic advance and retard. Solex carburetter. Clutch, single dry plate type.

ELECTRICAL EQUIPMENT. 6-volt lighting and starting set. Finger-tip control above steering wheel for dimming head lamps.

GEAR BOX. A three-speed box is fitted. This type provides silent second gear. The constant and second speed gears are of the double helical type ensuring silence and easy gear change. Gear ratios : Top, 5.22-1. Second, 9.61-1. First, 19.05-1. Reverse, 26.98-1.

PROPELLER SHAFT. Tubular type of large diameter, having two all-metal Universal joints.

REAR AXLE. Spiral bevel type, with a bevel type differential. The axle casing is of the banjo type, all parts very accessible.

FRONT AXLE. H-section beam, considerably dropped to allow of low built car.

BRAKES. Bendix Duo Servo. Both foot and hand brakes operate on all four wheels.

STEERING. Worm and nut type, giving a pleasantly light steering. The turning circle of the "Little Nine" is excellent, being 34 feet.

SPRINGS. Generous half-elliptic springing. Front 27½″ × 1½″. Rear 39″ × 1″. Hartford friction type shock absorbers fitted to front and rear axles.

PETROL SUPPLY. By Autovac from a 5-gallon tank carried at rear of chassis. A two way reserve petrol tap is provided giving a reserve supply of ¾ gallon.

WHEELS AND TYRES. Magna type wire wheels. Dunlop tyres, 27″ × 4″.

GENERAL DIMENSIONS. Wheelbase, 7′ 6″. Track, 3′ 8″. Height, 5′ 3″. Overall length, 10′ 10½″. (Special Model with bumpers, 11′ 4¼″). Weight 13 cwts. Width, 4′ 5″.

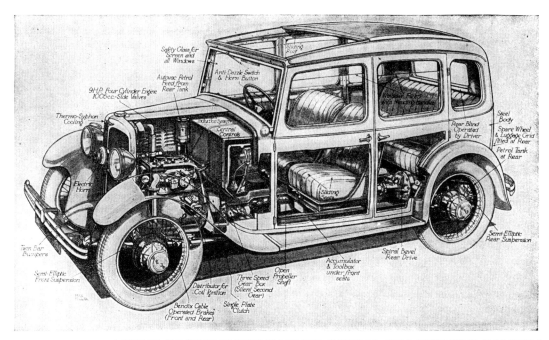

SECTIONAL DRAWING OF THE "LITTLE NINE" SPECIAL COACHBUILT SALOON

Copyright of "The Autocar."

The chassis of the 1932 Standard "Big Nine": the rear axle is of the spiral bevel type. All gear boxes have 4 speeds with silent third.

THE STANDARD 'BIG NINE'

BRIEF CHASSIS SPECIFICATION.

ENGINE. Four cylinder. 63.5 m/m bore, 102 m/m stroke. 1287 c.c. Tax £10. Side valves. Exceptionally stiff crankshaft, two bearing type, 1¾" diameter, front main bearing, 2¼" diameter rear, 1¾" diameter big ends, both dynamically and statically balanced. Aluminium pistons. Duralumin connecting rods. Detachable cylinder head. Lubrication by gear type pump, supplying oil under pressure to main bearings of crankshaft, camshaft, and to big ends. All oil passages are drilled integral with cylinder block. A float in the sump indicates quantity of oil, while pressure is recorded by gauge on dash. Ignition by coil and battery. Solex carburetter. Clutch, single dry plate type.

ELECTRICAL EQUIPMENT. 12-volt lighting and starting set. Finger-tip control above steer-ing wheel for dip switch, head lamps, also side lamps and charging.

GEAR BOX. A four speed box is fitted. This type provides silent third gear. The constant and third speed gears are of the double helical type ensuring silence and easy gear change. Gear ratios: Top, 5.33-1. Third, 7.01-1. Second, 11.03-1. First, 18.87-1. Reverse, 18.87-1.

PROPELLER SHAFT. Tubular type of large diameter, having two all-metal Universal joints.

REAR AXLE. Spiral bevel type, having four satellites in a bevel type differential. The axle casing is of the banjo type, all parts very accessible.

FRONT AXLE. H-section beam, considerably dropped to allow of low built car.

BRAKES. Bendix Duo Servo. Both foot and hand brakes operate on all four wheels.
STEERING. Marles-Weller cam and lever type, giving a pleasantly light steering. The turning circle of the "Big Nine" is excellent being 36 feet.
SPRINGS. Generous half-elliptic springing. Front 31¼"×1½". Rear 42"×1½". Luvax Hydraulic type shock absorbers fitted to front and rear axles.
PETROL SUPPLY. By petrol pump from a 9-gallon tank carried at rear of chassis. Electric petrol gauge visible on instrument board.
WHEELS AND TYRES. Magna type wire wheels. Dunlop tyres, 27"×4.40".
GENERAL DIMENSIONS. Wheelbase, 8' 4¼". Track, 4' 0". Height, 5' 8". Overall length, 12' 0". (Special Model with bumpers, 12' 6"). Weight 19¾ cwts. Width, 5' 1".

The chassis of the 1932 Standard "Sixteen": Bendix brakes are fitted, and Marles-Weller steering.

THE STANDARD 'SIXTEEN'

BRIEF CHASSIS SPECIFICATION.

ENGINE. Six cylinder. 65.5 m/m bore × 102 m/m stroke. 2054 c.c. Tax £16. Side valves. Exceptionally stiff crankshaft, seven bearing type, 2" diameter main bearings, 1¾" diameter big end, dynamically and statically balanced. Aluminium pistons. Duralumin connecting rods. Detachable cylinder head. Cooling system, Thermo syphon circulation of water assisted by a rotor driven from the same drive as the fan. Lubrication by gear type pump, supplying oil under pressure direct to main bearings of crankshaft, camshaft and to big ends. All oil passages are drilled integral with cylinder block. A float situated in the sump indicates quantity of oil, while pressure is recorded by gauge on dash. Special oil purifier is fitted in addition to usual filter. Chassis lubrication grease gun. Ignition by coil and battery. Clutch, single dry plate type. Solex carburetter.

ELECTRICAL EQUIPMENT. 12-volt lighting and starting set. Finger-tip control above steering wheel for dip-switch, head lamps, side lamps and charging.

GEAR BOX. In unit with engine, providing four forward speeds, silent third gear type. Constant and third speed gears are of the double helical type ensuring silence and easy gear change Central control. Gear ratios: Top, 5.11-1. Third, 6.72-1. Second, 10.59-1. First, 18.1-1. Reverse, 18.1-1.

PROPELLER SHAFT. Tubular type of large diameter, having two all-metal Universal joints.

REAR AXLE. Spiral bevel type, having four satellites in a bevel type differential. The axle casing is of the banjo type, all parts very accessible.

FRONT AXLE. H-section beams, considerably dropped to allow of low built car.

BRAKES. Bendix Duo Servo. Both foot and hand brakes operate on all four wheels.
STEERING. Marles-Weller cam and lever type, giving a pleasantly light steering. Turning circle, 38 feet.
SPRINGS. Generous half-elliptic springing. Front springs, 32"×1½". Rear, 42"×1½". Luvax Hydraulic shock absorbers fitted front and rear.
PETROL SUPPLY. By A.C. Pump from 9-gallon tank carried at the rear of the chassis. The pump is driven by the same gears as the engine oil pump ; visible filter is provided. An electrically operated petrol gauge is fitted in the instrument board.
WHEELS AND TYRES. Magna type wire wheels. Dunlop tyres, 29"×5".
GENERAL DIMENSIONS. Wheelbase, 9' 1". Track, 4' 0". Overall length, 13' 0". (Special Model with bumper bars, 13' 6"). Width, 5' 1". Height, 5' 8".

KV 641

1933—THE FINEST SUMMER FOR 30 YEARS!

YES ! This year the finest summer you've ever had awaits you. Whatever the weather ! Because a new kind of motoring is ready for you. *Standard* motoring — so different from ordinary motoring. There's only six cars in the world that can provide this silken care-free motoring. Made by Standard in the very heart of England, the 1933 Standards —successful products of British skill and labour—are at your service !

(*Above*). This is the new Standard " Little Twelve " — brilliant favourite of sparkling capabilities ; built on the lines of the 1933 Standard " Little Nine " yet with the added power and performance of an exceptionally efficient six-cylinder engine, developing 29 brake horsepower with an R.A.C. rating of 12 h.p.

1933 STANDARD CARS

THEY LOOK SUCCESSFUL — *and they are!*

This is the Standard "Big Nine" Special Saloon — the car which built the Standard reputation, in its 1933 form.

EVERY STANDARD CAR FOR 1933 HAS—

Flush-fitting sliding roof.

Four speed silent third gearbox.

Grouped nipple chassis lubrication.

Self-start carburettor.

12 volt lighting and starting set.

Hydraulic shock absorbers, etc.

Yet not only have they lavish equipment but superb capabilities and appearance also. See them and read about them in the 1933 catalogue. Just write "Catalogue" on a postcard and post it with your name and address to:—The Standard Motor Company Ltd., Canley, Coventry. West End Showrooms: The Car Mart Ltd., 46-50 Park Lane, London, W.1, and 297-9 Euston Road, London, N.W.1.

Read "The Standard Car Review," published monthly, subscription 3/6 a year post free.

1933 STANDARD CARS

FIVE SPLENDID NEW CARS—

*accurately adjusted to the needs of motorists to-day;
equipped with all the latest features of the costliest car
practice, including—*

ENTIRELY NEW BODYWORK OF UNIQUE DESIGN
Far roomier and much more beautiful.   (No foot wells)

* *

BUOYANT POWER
(New and scientific resilient engine mounting)

* *

RE-DESIGNED BENDIX BRAKES
Light in action, progressively powerful, skid-free

* *

**SYNCHRO-MESH GEARS IN SECOND, THIRD AND TOP
COMBINED WITH CONTROLLED FREE-WHEELING**
Giving absolutely silent, lightning changes

* *

STARTIX AUTOMATIC RE-STARTING

* *

X-BRACED FRAMES
Underslung on 9 and 10 h.p. models

* *

ILLUMINATED DIRECTION INDICATORS
Self-cancelling and flush-fitting

* *

**SLIDING ROOF WITH ONE POINT
OPERATION**

* *

**THERMOSTATICALLY CONTROLLED WATER
TEMPERATURE**

* *

SILENT-BLOC SHACKLES
(No spring shackles to lubricate)

* *

TWO SYNCHRONISED SCREEN WIPERS
With concealed silent motor

* *

NO-DRAUGHT DOOR WINDOW LOUVRES

* *

CENTRAL WINDSCREEN CONTROL
Infinitely variable

* *

**CONCEALED SPARE WHEEL AND
LUGGAGE GRID**
Eliminating removal of spare wheel for washing car

* *

COMPENSATED VOLTAGE CONTROL

* *

**D.W.S. INTEGRAL FOUR-WHEEL JACKING
SYSTEM**
On 16 and 20 h.p. models.   (Other models supplied with
accessible pads placed at front and rear for easy operation)

*A new completer silence, higher speed, faster acceleration,
better hill-climbing abilities, even greater reliability!*

ENTIRELY NEW BODYWORK OF UNIQUE DESIGN

The bodywork of the 1934 Standards is of entirely new design, giving much greater comfort and accommodation and unrestricted entrance and exit. Body lines are lower and more sweeping, and cunningly streamlined. The sliding roof is instantly operated and locked by a single lever. The single panel windscreen, fitted with Triplex toughened glass, is centrally controlled and infinitely variable. Seats are richly upholstered in finest quality furniture hide or leather cloth, in suitable tones to harmonise with the exterior colour schemes. No footwells are fitted as ample leg room renders them unnecessary. Illuminated direction indicators, flush-fitting and self-cancelling, are supplied, also no-draught door window louvres integral with the body. The rear window is fitted with blind, operated from driver's seat. Interior lights are controlled by independent switches on each pillar.

This is the 1934 " Nine "—an entirely new production ! A full four-seater two-door saloon for £135 ! Equipped with underslung and X-braced chassis frame ensuring remarkable rigidity and road-holding ; " Buoyant Power " resilient engine mounting ; and synchro-mesh silent gears in second, third and top.

The very popular Standard "Sixteen" has been increased in size, and a full five-seater four-door, six-light body is now fitted.

ROADWORTHINESS
—a positive revelation!

Standard springing and stability, always excellent, are now a positive revelation! 1934 chassis are fitted with a substantial cruciform-bracing to frames, eliminating all tendency to whip and banishing front end movement. 1934 nine and ten horse-power chassis are underslung, the centre of gravity being extremely low. The springs are longer and wider, with lower periodicity. Silentbloc shackles are fitted, removing the need for lubrication. And safety? Even greater than ever, with redesigned Bendix brakes—light in action, progressively powerful, skid-free! Truly, the 1934 Standard cars are built to the uncompromising commands of minds that know just what the public *want!*

The interior of the 1934 Standard "Twelve" showing the amazing roominess of the body.

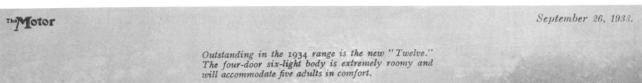

Outstanding in the 1934 range is the new "Twelve."
The four-door six-light body is extremely roomy and
will accommodate five adults in comfort.

BUOYANT POWER

The new and scientific resilient engine mounting.

It is when you switch on the engine and begin to drive that you are most acutely conscious of the wonderful qualities of these unique cars. *No vibration!* You *cannot* believe that an exceptionally efficient and amply powerful engine has leapt into life beneath the bonnet before you. That's *Buoyant Power*, the new and scientific engine mounting which absorbs every trace of vibration which the engine creates, insulating it from the car itself. Thus the 1934 Standards provide a new, completer silence. Every driving sound is hushed, every quietening device employed, from the streamlining of the roof to reduce the noise of air eddies at speed, to the fitting of the new and silent lift cams.

This is the 1934 Standard "Ten." A car with a 10 h.p. three-bearing four-cylinder engine, developing 32 brake h.p. at 3,600 revs. Fitted with an exceptionally roomy four-door six-light body, it gives a road performance which is quite amazing.

SYNCHRO-MESH GEARS IN SECOND, 3rd AND TOP COMBINED WITH CONTROLLED FREE-WHEELING

The 1934 Standards have synchro-mesh gears in second, third and top, combined with controlled free-wheeling, giving more silent and faster changes than any you have known before! Petrol consumption is improved . . . and a new and thrilling road performance is added to Standard steadiness and reliability—higher speed, faster acceleration, greater hill-climbing abilities! All bodies are fitted with the latest form of instrument panel. (*See illustration above on left.*) The two synchronised windscreen wipers are operated by a concealed and silent motor. The 1934 Standards are equipped with Startix Automatic Re-starting. Compensated voltage control dynamo is *entirely new and automatic.* Water temperature is thermostatically controlled. New harmonically-tuned electric horns are fitted of a design to harmonise with the whole decorative scheme. Reversing lamps are added to certain models. Windscreen wipers, and all exposed parts (including wings, and safety steel running boards) are rust resisting. D W S Four-wheel Jacking system is supplied on 16 and 20 h.p. models (other models fitted with accessible pads at front and rear for easy operation).

Reprinted from The Autocar April 6th, 1934.

"THE AUTOCAR" ROAD TESTS

TEN-TWELVE STANDARD SPEED SALOON

No. 851 (*Post-War Series*)

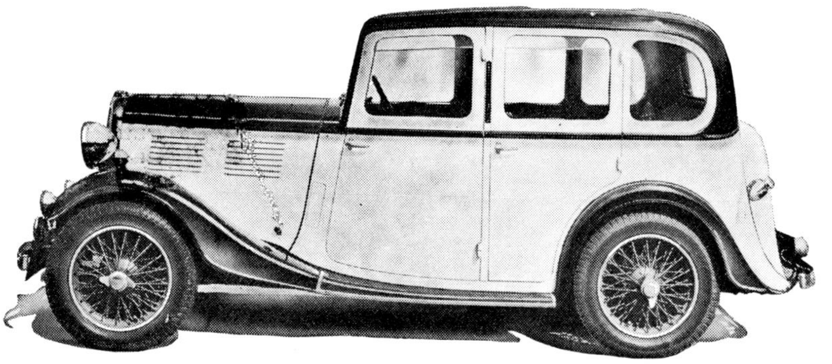

First-rate Performance of an "Innocent-looking" Car Which is Fairly Light in Weight and Has a Reasonably Large Four-cylinder Engine

BY the simple expedient of putting a 12 h.p. four-cylinder engine into a normal type of 10 h.p. Standard saloon, and strengthening up things wherever necessary, a decidedly remarkable car has been created. It has a smart and innocent appearance, but a performance which would be very creditable to a small open sports car.

A genuine timed speed, the average of runs with and against the wind, of 70 m.p.h. is definitely remarkable for a 12 h.p. four-seater saloon with plenty of headroom and a perfectly comfortable interior, with all the equipment in place. Not less remarkable is the ability to reach 50 m.p.h. from a standing start in sixteen seconds.

This car creates a new standard in saloons of the smaller kind, for it combines the comfort of a full four-seater closed car, most thoroughly equipped and suitable to be driven by any member of the family because of its easy controllability, with an ability to cruise effortlessly at 60 m.p.h., and to put up an average speed of 40 m.p.h. over long distances without appearing to be exerting any effort. The reason is that the car is fairly light and has a fairly large engine, although the tax, insurance, and fuel consumption are relatively small items.

Few 16 h.p. six-cylinder cars can boast a road performance as good. The 10-12 h.p. Standard will climb a long 1 in 10 gradient on top gear at well over 30 m.p.h., and will tackle a well-known 1 in 9 test hill, with a right-angle corner approach, at 36 m.p.h. on top or 43 m.p.h. on third. On the Test Hill at Brooklands it is possible to change up into second after a standing start, and average practically 20 m.p.h. for the climb.

Although this latest Standard model has a performance of such real snap, it is perfectly pleasant to handle, and need not be driven fast. It is quite docile, and still gets over the ground quickly even if driven comparatively gently, because it gets back into its stride so easily and quickly after slowing down for traffic, corners, and so forth. It sits steadily on the road throughout its speed range, and will negotiate curves fast and comfortably because of its low chassis.

The steering is light and definite, the car is easy to manœuvre in a garage, and also is quite happy when travelling fast over a steeply cambered road, so that there is no sense of strain when passing another car at speed. The brakes are in keeping with the performance; the pedal does not need a heavy pressure, and the degree of slowing down is progressive according to the pressure applied. No tendency to wander under heavy braking was noticed when testing the emergency stopping distance from 30 m.p.h.

Fitted with an aluminium cylinder head, giving a high compression, and twin Solex carburetters, the three-bearing crankshaft, side-valve engine runs smoothly, as well as producing plenty of power, and by reason of its rubber mounting in the frame could easily be mistaken for a six during most of its working range. It is flexible, able to pull hard at low speeds, and not inclined to "pink" on ordinary fuels. It gives the car a fine top gear range from a genuine walking speed up to the maximum. The car will do nearly all its work on top gear, but, of course, use of the gear box will give still more vivid results.

The maximum on second gear is 38 m.p.h., and on third 55 m.p.h. The gear box is very quiet on the indirects, and the provision of synchromesh for second, third and top reduces gear changing to a simple matter of pushing out the clutch and pulling the gear lever slowly and evenly into the next position, without bothering much about the use of the accelerator pedal except to lift it. A controlled free wheel is fitted, and, if it be used, gear changing may be accomplished merely by releasing the accelerator, and not using the clutch, whilst the gear lever is moved.

TEN-TWELVE STANDARD SPEED SALOON

DATA FOR THE DRIVER

10-12 h.p., four cylinders, 69.5 × 106 mm. (1,608.5 c.c.). Tax £12.
Tyres: 4.75 × 17in. on knock-off wire wheels.

Engine—rear axle gear ratios.	Acceleration from steady speed. 10 to 30 m.p.h.	20 to 40 m.p.h.	30 to 50 m.p.h.	Timed speed over ¼ mile.
19.18 to 1	—	—	—	
11.8 to 1	5⅗ sec.	—	—	
7.06 to 1	6⅗ sec.	7⅘ sec.	10⅕ sec.	
4.86 to 1	9⅗ sec.	9⅖ sec.	11⅗ sec.	70.31 m.p.h.

Acceleration from rest through the gears to 50 m.p.h., 16 sec.
Speed up Brooklands Test Hill from rest (1 in 5 average gradient), 19.69 m.p.h. (on first and second gears).
15 yards of 1 in 5 gradient from rest, 3 sec.
Turning circle: 36ft.
Tank capacity 8 gallons, fuel consumption 22-24 m.p.g.
12-volt lighting set cuts in at 12 m.p.h.; automatic dynamo voltage control.
Weight: 20 cwt. 1 qr.
Price, with saloon body, £245.

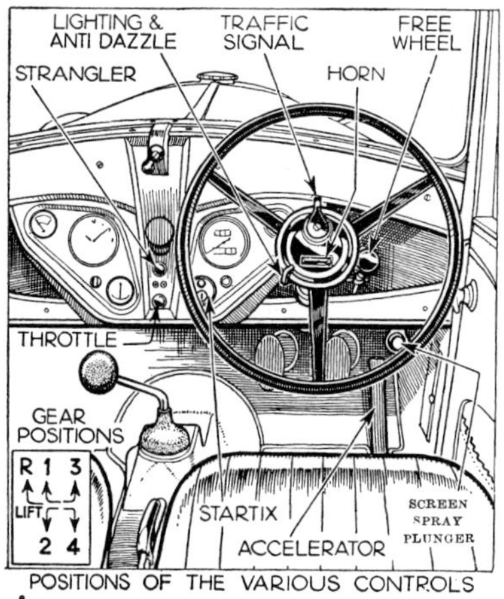
LIGHTING & ANTI DAZZLE
TRAFFIC SIGNAL
FREE WHEEL
STRANGLER
HORN
THROTTLE
GEAR POSITIONS
R 1 3
LIFT
2 4
STARTIX
ACCELERATOR
SCREEN SPRAY PLUNGER

POSITIONS OF THE VARIOUS CONTROLS

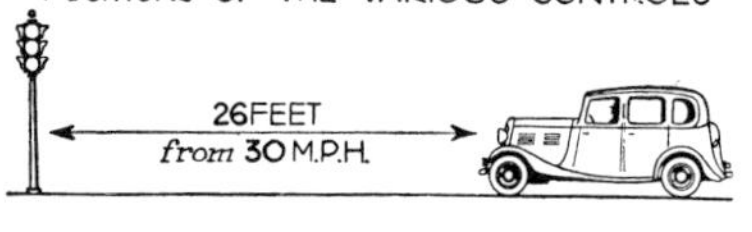
26FEET
from 30 M.P.H.

Printed in Great Britain by The Cornwall Press Ltd., Paris Garden, London, S.E.1.

"THE AUTOCAR" ROAD TESTS

TEN-TWELVE STANDARD SPEED SALOON

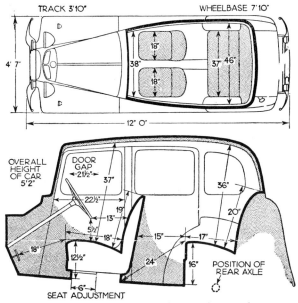

Incidentally, the whole car is quiet running, engine, gears, and coachwork as well, and though that may not seem to be a comment of particular value to make in connection with a comparatively new car, it is by no means always possible to offer it.

There is a surprising amount of room in the compact body. This is due to the dropped frame, which gives a low floor level, and permits the seats to be set at a reasonable height, whilst still retaining as much head room as anyone needs. The front seats are separate and immediately adjustable, and when tall people occupy them there is still plenty of leg room in the back, for a great deal of extra toe room is given by hollows that are formed underneath the front seats.

The driving position is comfortable, for the wheel is not too high, and the controls could hardly be more conveniently arranged and placed, from the piano-type accelerator pedal to the horizontally disposed central brake lever, and the self-cancelling Trafficator control, lamp switches, and horn button on the pleasingly thin-rimmed steering wheel.

Altogether, this new 10-12 h.p. Standard speed saloon is a remarkable car, and one which should exactly suit those people who wish to get about the country really quickly, but easily, in comfort, and in an inconspicuous fashion. There must be many such motorists who, together with their families, appreciate the sound, sensible qualities of the ordinary type of car as far as appearance and seating space go, yet at times—even if not as a habit—have a liking and practical uses for snappy acceleration, and an easily maintained cruising speed of a distinctly useful order, such as this Standard undoubtedly can provide.

Finally, the car appears able to repeat its performance figures without variation, and does not need favourable circumstances in order to do well. The car tested took part in the R.A.C. Bournemouth Rally, and it had covered in all 2,300 miles since being put into commission.

STANDARD SPEED 10·12

The STANDARD

Clearly Defined Range of 9, 10, 12, 16 an
and Advantageou

New engine mounting with rubber-cushioned steady bracket on the near side of the Twelve engine.

IMPROVEMENTS of considerable moment to the owner are incorporated in the range of Standard cars for 1936, which substantially is unchanged in scope in that it caters for all needs, from the simplest form of two-door 9 h.p. saloon at a modest price right up to the luxurious long-wheelbase 20 h.p. seven-seater saloon.

The range, however, has been simplified as compared with last year, and, with the sole exception of the lowest-priced 9 h.p. model, all the cars have a complete de luxe equipment. It has

been found that Standard car owners in the main are apt to pass over lower-priced types with less ambitious equipment, and to go straight for the best obtainable. Advantage has been taken of this fact to reduce the number of models which differed only in equipment.

There is, however, another aspect of Standard activity which inevitably must be reflected in the cars themselves. In pursuit of the goal of quality which is the main endeavour of the works

Nine.—9 h.p., four cylinders, 60.3×92 mm. (1,052 c.c.). Tax £6 15s. Wheelbase 6ft. 10in., track 3ft. 10in., overall length 11ft. 9in., width 4ft. 7in., height 5ft. 2in. Two-door saloon £135; two-door saloon de luxe £155.

Nine.—Four-door saloon, wheelbase 7ft. 3½in., overall length 12ft. 1in., £169.

Ten.—10 h.p., four cylinders, 63.5×106 mm. (1,343 c.c.). Tax £7 10s. Wheelbase 7ft. 7in., track 4ft., overall length 12ft. 4in., width 4ft. 10in., height 5ft. 2in. Saloon £189.

Light Twelve.—11.98 h.p., four cylinders, 69.5×106 mm. (1,608.5 c.c.). Tax £9. Other particulars as for Ten saloon. £195.

Twelve.—11.98 h.p., four cylinders, 69.5×106 mm. (1,608.5 c.c.). Tax £9. Wheelbase 8ft. 3in.,

The two-door four-light Nine.

track 4ft. 4in., overall length 13ft. 4in., width 5ft. 1in., height 5ft. 7in. Saloon £229.

Sixteen.—15.96 h.p., six cylinders, 65.5×106 mm. (2,143 c.c.). Tax £12. Wheelbase 8ft. 11in., track 4ft. 8in., overall length 14ft., width 5ft. 5in., height 5ft. 7in. Saloon £269.

Light Twenty.—19.84 h.p., six cylinders, 73×106 mm. (2,663.7 c.c.). Tax £15. Other particulars as for Sixteen. Saloon £275.

Twenty.—19.84 h.p., six cylinders, 73×106 mm. (2,663.7 c.c.). Tax £15. Wheelbase 9ft. 9in. or 10ft. 3in., track 4ft. 9½in., overall length 14ft. 6in. or 15ft. 6in., width 5ft. 10in., height 5ft. 10in. Saloon, seven seats, £395; saloon, long wheelbase, £450.

Commenting on the foregoing, it may be mentioned that the two-door and four-door Nines, the Ten, the Twelve, and the Sixteen show price reductions, whilst the Light Twelve is approximately the same car as the Ten, but with a large engine, and takes the place of the Ten-Twelve of last year, but is not a speed model in the sense of special tuning.

To deal next with the changes and improvements which have been adopted: in the first place the coachwork has come in for very little revision, which is as might be expected, for the Standard bodies of the last few years have—writing from experience—been remarkably good, and free from rattles, squeaks, draughts, and the other small ailments liable to afflict the user with growing mileage.

A new instrument panel has been adopted, with combined instruments having cream faces illuminated from be-

Four-door six-light Sixteen saloon.

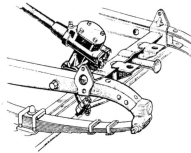

The steering box on the Twelve is well forward and high up.

team, the factory recently has been reorganised along the most modern lines of efficient production, and large new shops have been built and carefully equipped to ensure not only regularity of production flow, but also regularity of a high standard. The factory is now able to deal with an increased rate of manufacture into the bargain. As a result of these forward steps the economy of production is improved, whence it follows that slight reductions in price become possible, or, conversely, more can be given for the same money.

The full list of the 1936 Standard cars and their prices is as follows:—

PROGRAMME

20 h.p. Models, With Considerable Improvements
adjustments of Price

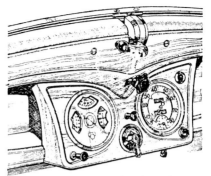

Neat instrument panel and windscreen operation on the Standard Ten.

easier to clean. In the sides of the bonnet horizontal fine louvres are grouped in a distinctive design.

From the mechanical point of view there are many features to record. Primarily, the change in frontal appearance already mentioned is chiefly due to a mechanical improvement. The engine has been moved farther for-

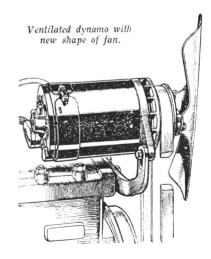

Four-door Nine saloon.

The four-door Ten from above.

hind, and a large-dial speedometer with the 30 m.p.h. limit mark clearly indicated. Then the arrangement of the minor controls has been altered. In the centre of the steering wheel are the horn button, the traffic indicator switch, and the switch for the head lamp dip control, whilst the switch for lights and charging is now mounted on the instrument panel.

Outwardly, the new cars have a somewhat different frontal appearance, for the radiator is mounted in modern fashion far forward, and at a slope so that it meets the forward edge of the wings. The wings themselves are of a new design, and are deeper fronted, whilst head lamps of a more streamline shape are mounted farther forward and lower than before.

The wing valances meet the bonnet sides, and bonnet boards are abolished, so that the front of the car should be

ward so as to alter the weight distribution and make it possible to use front springs which in periodicity match the rear suspension more closely, so that pitching is very considerably reduced, and a "flat-ride" results.

Burman-Douglas steering gear is fitted on the Nine, Ten, Light 12 h.p. and 12 h.p. cars, and is specially designed to deal with the more flexible front springs so that definiteness of steering is retained. The gear is mounted far forward, and a transverse drag link used, so that the steering column is in a more horizontal position, and the full value obtained for the telescopic adjustment fore and aft of the steering wheel itself. Another important improvement concerns the chassis frames, which have been rendered more rigid in construction and have most of the brackets welded in place.

During the current year considerable improvement was made to the "buoyant power" floating type of rubber suspension for the power unit on Standard cars, the rubber bush cushions being changed to flat pads set at an angle, so that the engine rests in a V, and, in addition on the near side, an extra controlling buffer was introduced. These features made a great improvement at the low speed end of the range in a system which is so effective as to make it

difficult to tell from inside the car whether the engine has four or six cylinders.

For 1936 the engines themselves have received further development; the machined combustion chambers have been improved in shape, and a downdraught carburetter is fitted to a new hotspot inlet manifold, the result being a considerable gain in power, and therefore in acceleration, without detracting from smoothness or strong pulling at slow speeds. Another point is that the latest type of ventilated dynamo is now

Ventilated dynamo with new shape of fan.

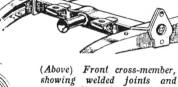

The Standard Programme

fitted, which runs at a lower temperature and gives a more efficient output.

On the Nine engine also—which has a 12-volt lighting set—the capacity of the oil sump has been increased, and on all models the exhaust silencing system has been improved and provided with flexible mountings. The Ten, Twelve, Sixteen and Twenty engines now have a thermostat control of water temperature provided with a by-pass pipe to give rapid warming up from cold.

On the Ten and Light Twelve the track has been increased by 2in., which allows a similar increase in the width of the rear seat within the body. On all models an excellent four-speed gear box fitted with synchromesh on second, third and top gear for easy gear changing is incorporated. The synchromesh was recently greatly improved in its action, and the gear lever responds readily to light movement, so that it is next door

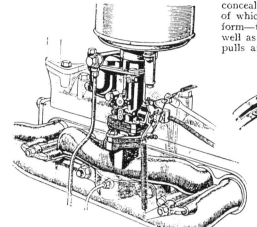

concealed in a built-in container—the lid of which opens to form a luggage platform—telescopic steering adjustment as well as adjustable seats, ash trays, rope pulls and various other smaller details.

(Above) Front cross-member, showing welded joints and radiator brackets.

(Left) Inlet pipe and new downdraught carburetter on the Ten.

Lastly, there is a wider choice of improved colour schemes.

Road Impressions

Advantage was taken of an opportunity to make trial runs over a short but familiar test course with 1936 examples from the production line of the Nine two-door de luxe saloon and the Ten de luxe saloon.

The first observation to make as a result is, perhaps, a queer one. The cars are very water-tight! The reason for the remark is that during the summer afternoon in question, on both occasions, the centre of a terrific thunderstorm-cum-cloudburst was entered, with rain so torrential that even a weather-hardened car-tester had to stop for lack of visibility. But no water entered the bodies, which can by no means be said of all modern coachwork, including expensive cars. However, that is scarcely a leading impression, though a point well worthy of emphasis.

One of the first points to be noticed is the improvement in the comfort of the springing which results from the altered weight distribution. Both cars ride well and smoothly, even over bad roads, with a minimum of pitching. The suspension is unusually smooth and is such as to give the feeling of riding in a large car.

Next, it is apparent that the engines run particularly quietly and very smoothly indeed ; nevertheless, they develop appreciably more power, so that acceleration and hill-climbing are both very good. These engines certainly run like rather nicely balanced electric motors, with just a faint whirring sound, and at the lowest speeds the floating mounting of the power unit does not become obtrusively slack. The steering of the two cars proves pleasantly light, even when turning on full lock at slow speeds. There is a very marked improvement, too, in the gear change, for the latest synchromesh makes the movement of the gear lever much lighter, and it is easier than previously to get out of one gear before moving the lever over to the next.

These two cars are very pleasant to drive, or to be driven in, for the seats are comfortable, the driving position is capable of adjustment to suit individuals of widely varying build, there is good visibility, adequate control of ventilation, an entire absence of fumes, plenty of headroom, ease of entry, and an interior finish of a quality to take the eye.

Standard Ten four-door six-light saloon.

to impossible to find difficulty in obtaining silent and easy gear changing. Free wheels are no longer fitted, as the new synchromesh makes them redundant.

The gear box is fitted with a dipstick to make it easy to check the oil level, and this dipstick is now so arranged that it can be used without moving the floor mats. Incidentally, a draught- and heat-proof floor covering is a great feature of Standard coachwork, so that heat, fumes or draughts are very well excluded from the interior of the particularly comfortable and neatly trimmed coachwork.

Easy Jacking System

An easy jacking system is fitted to all models; on the 9, 10 and 12 h.p. cars it is effected by a ratchet- and handle-operated square-thread jack post, which can instantaneously be clipped on to suitable sockets provided in the bumper bar brackets.

It has been mentioned that de luxe equipment is provided on all models except the Nine. It is, therefore, important to note the implication of this comprehensive term. The equipment in-

cludes safety glass throughout, furniture hide upholstery, chromium-plated lamps, sliding roof, centre winding screen, twin concealed wipers, anti-draught louvres over the windows, pile carpets with draught-proof underlays, the spare wheel

The new radiator is more imposing.

Two Standard cars from the same period, with the lower picture showing Prince Philip's old 1935 two-door "Nine".

THE TWO-DOOR "NINE"

The Standard Two-door "Nine" has been designed to sell, at the lowest possible price, a thoroughly roadworthy car, capable of seating four people in ample comfort. Maximum speed 60 m.p.h. 12-volt lighting and starting. Four-speed synchro-mesh gearbox. Down-draught carburetter. Chassis underslung at rear.

TWO-DOOR SALOON - - **£135**
TWO-DOOR SALOON DE LUXE **£155**

THE FOUR-DOOR "NINE"

This car differs only from the Two-door "Nine" de luxe in its longer wheelbase, and four-door body. Equipped with a superb array of features, common to the whole Standard range, including "Buoyant Power" engine mounting and 12-volt lighting and starting set. The "Nine" is built to be the most efficient car of its size.

FOUR-DOOR SALOON DE LUXE **£169**

THE "TEN" and "LIGHT TWELVE"

A light car in the truest sense of the word—roomy seating, low in first cost, and extremely economical in tax, insurance, petrol consumption and tyre wear. A very gratifying performance. Telescopic steering column for adjustment to personal liking, thermostat-controlled water temperature with pump circulation, draught-free window louvres, etc., etc.

"TEN" SALOON DE LUXE - - **£189**
"LIGHT TWELVE" SALOON DE LUXE **£195**

THE "TWELVE"

Superb roadholding, comfort and responsiveness, resulting from this car's substantial dimensions, coupled with many important improvements common to the new Standard range—cross-braced chassis frame, welded joints, box section at front end, engine forward for better weight distribution, and long springs of lower periodicity controlled by Luvax Hydraulic Shock Absorbers. Brilliant performance and "big car" accommodation.

SALOON DE LUXE - - **£229**

THE "SIXTEEN" and "LIGHT TWENTY"

A roomy, stylish, handsome car with a very fine six-cylinder engine with seven-bearing crankshaft and machined combustion chambers. D.W.S. four-wheel permanent jacking system, sumptuous perfection of equipment and finish throughout, and a very fine performance place the "Sixteen" in a luxury class far above its price.

"SIXTEEN" SALOON DE LUXE - **£269**
"LIGHT TWENTY" SALOON DE LUXE **£275**

THE "TWENTY"

While most cars of this size and performance are suitable only for the professional driver, this model has such light and perfectly balanced controls that many women motorists are regular and enthusiastic drivers of Standard "Twenties." 70 m.p.h. and ample accommodation for seven people.

SHORT WHEELBASE SALOON DE LUXE **£395**
LONG WHEELBASE SALOON DE LUXE **£450**

1936 MODELS AND PRICES

9 h.p. Two-door Saloon - -	**£135**

ALL DE LUXE MODEL PROGRAMME.

9 h.p. Two-door Saloon - -	**£155**
9 h.p. Four-door Saloon - -	**£169**
10 ,, ,, ,, -	**£189**
"Light Twelve" Saloon - -	**£195**
"Twelve" Saloon - - -	**£229**
"Sixteen" Saloon - - -	**£269**
"Light Twenty" Saloon - -	**£275**
"Twenty" S.W.B. Saloon - -	**£395**
,, L.W.B. Saloon - -	**£450**

All prices ex works.
Triplex Toughened Glass.   Dunlop Tyres.

BRIEF CHASSIS SPECIFICATIONS

DATA	2-DOOR NINE & 4-DOOR NINE	TEN	LIGHT TWELVE	TWELVE	SIXTEEN	LIGHT TWENTY	TWENTY L.W.B.
Tax	£6-15-0	£7-10-0	£9-0-0	£9-0-0	£12-0-0	£15-0-0	£15-0-0
Number of cyls.	4	4	4	4	6	6	6
Bore & stroke, mm.	60.3×92	63.5×106	69.5×106	69.5×106	65.5×106	73×106	73×106
Capacity c.c.	1052	1343	1608.5	1608.5	2143	2663.7	2663.7
Number of crank bearings	2	3	3	3	7	7	7
Battery voltage	12	12	12	12	12	12	12
Carburetter	Zenith Downdraught	Solex Downdraught	Solex Downdraught	Solex Downdraught	Solex Downdraught	Solex Downdraught	Solex Downdraught
Petrol Tank Capacity (Galls.) [2-Door / 4-Door]	7 / 8	8	8	10	10	10	15
Gear ratios—Top....	5.43 / 5.57	5.43	4.86	5.375	5.25	4.75	4.89
3rd....	7.38 / 8.09	7.88	7.06	7.81	7.20	6.52	6.71
2nd....	13.18 / 13.53	13.18	11.80	13.05	11.10	10.04	10.34
1st....	21.42 / 21.99	21.42	19.18	21.2	18.90	17.10	17.60
Dimensions—Tyre size .... [2-Door / 4-Door]	4.5—17 / 4.5—17	4.75—17	4.75—17	5—17	5.5—17	5.5—17	6.00—17
Wheelbase	6'10" / 7'3¼"	7'7"	7'7"	8'3"	8'11"	8'11"	10'3"
Track	3'10" / 3'10"	4'0"	4'0"	4'4"	4'8"	4'8"	4'9½"
Ground clearance (under axle)....	7¾" / 7¾"	7¾"	7¾"	7½"	8"	8"	8½"
Length	11'9" / 12'1"	12'4"	12'4"	13'4"	14'0"	14'0"	15'6"
Width	4'7" / 4'7"	4'10"	4'10"	5'1"	5'5"	5'5"	5'10"
Height	5'2" / 5'2"	5'2"	5'2"	5'7"	5'7"	5'7"	5'9"
Weight	16½ cwt. / 17½ cwt.	19¼ cwt.	19¼ cwt.	23 cwt.	26 cwt.	26 cwt.	32½ cwt.

For full specifications, terms of business and six months' guarantee, see separate lists.

THE STANDARD MOTOR CO., LTD., CANLEY, COVENTRY

THE NEW STANDARDS

Here is a new series of Standard cars that, point for point, no other cars of similar class can excel. Their horsepowers run from 9 to 20, prices from £135 to £450, but the difference is only in size and in equipment.

In these new models the engines have been improved to give greater power, reduced petrol consumption. They have new four-speed gearboxes—synchro-mesh on second, third and top—perfected to give absolutely smooth and silent changes throughout. The chassis are improved in many important ways that give wonderful road-holding, comfort and ease of control. Self-cancelling illuminated trafficators. A new and wonderfully comfortable position for the steering wheel, with telescopic steering column on the "Ten," "Light Twelve," " Twelve," " Sixteen " and " Light Twenty."

Improved interior fittings, wider seats. Oversize tyres giving extra mileage as well as greater comfort. And with it all, a completely new and bolder outline. A range of cars built " for motorists who put quality first."

1936 COLOUR SCHEMES

Body Colour	Wings	Wheels	Moulding	Lining	Trimming
Standard Colours—					
All Black	Black	Black	Black	Gold	Fawn
All Maroon	Black	Black	Black	Gold	New Maroon
All Peasant Blue	Black	Black	Black	Gold	Peasant Blue
New Condor Grey	Black	Black	Black	Gold	Fawn
All Green	Black	Black	Black	Gold	Green

De Luxe Models are finished in the following DUAL COLOURS :

Base	Top	Wings	Wheels	Lining	Trimming
Light Grey	Dark Grey	Dark Grey	Light Grey	Gold	Peasant Blue
Maroon	Black	Black	Black	Gold	New Maroon
New Condor Grey	Black	Black	Black	Gold	Fawn
Green	Black	Black	Black	Gold	Green
Peasant Blue	Black	Black	Black	Gold	Peasant Blue

Every precaution has been taken in the preparation of this booklet, but the Company cannot be responsible for any error or omission and reserve the right to alter or amend the specification without previous notice.

THE *Flying*

BRITISH - BUILT

Ample accommodation (for two large and two small suitcases) is provided in the two-compartment locker in the tail (which also holds tools and the spare wheel carried horizontally).

BUY A CAR MADE IN THE

Translucent illuminated instrument panel with gauges and meters neatly combined in one dial ; balanced by an extra large speedometer of similar size (30 m.p.h. specially marked) incorporating the clock.

'Flying 12' 4

'Flying 16'

'Flying 20'

STANDARD

OR MOTORISTS WHO PUT QUALITY FIRST !

KINGDOM

The chassis is low, long and especially rigid ; the sliding roof has self-locking central control ; the trafficators are self-cancelling and flush-fitting ; the wheels are fitted with detachable discs.

All seating is *within the wheelbase*. The " Flying Standard " provides accommodation for six — three on the one-piece adjustable front seat, three on the extra-wide (48 ins.) rear seat.

NDER **£259**

NDER **£299**

NDER **£315**

SS   ALL PRICES EX WORKS

A New Flying Avon Twenty Saloon

Highly Specialised Coachwork Provided with Almost Unlimited Luggage Capacity

MANY points of particular interest are to be found in the latest design by the New Avon Body Co., Ltd., for the 1937 Flying Twenty four-door saloon, which is priced at £375.

Not only is the car of striking and graceful appearance, but it is essentially practical in all its features, and has a very wide scope of utility for many motoring purposes. For example, it fills the bill for town use, being smart, quiet, very quick to accelerate, and especially spacious in the interior, besides easy to enter or leave by reason of the very wide doors, and the flat flooring without foot-wells.

Yet the car is equally suitable for the pursuit of open-air sports, for the provision for luggage or other equipment is perhaps the most comprehensive ever provided in a regularly produced car. For instance, four people may occupy the seats, but there is room in the luggage boot for four complete sets of golf bags, or several guns, fishing rods and other angling tackle, plus the waders, and so on. All can be stowed away safely and out of sight. But this is only the beginning of the accommodation.

If two people want to set out on a long tour they can take every bit as much luggage as they need, because there is a very special arrangement in the back part of the body. It is this. The squab and the rear seat cushion are vertically divided into two parts. When desired, each or both parts of the seat cushion may be lifted forward and folded down into the space above the floor. Then each or both parts of the squab can be folded forward and down until the squab, now face downwards, occupies the space vacated by the cushion. A flap hinged to the squab falls into place, and then there is a lug-

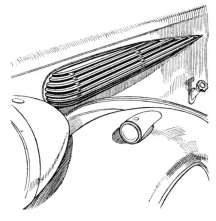

New form of bonnet louvre adds distinction to the appearance of the car.

gage platform provided inside the back of the car right from the lid of the boot forward to the backs of the front seats, a space measuring 57 by 41 by 30 inches. Moreover, this colossal luggage space is so arranged that when it is in use the upholstery of the seats is out of sight and out of harm's way.

But that is not all. If three people are to be carried, the empty fourth seat in the back can be converted to luggage space by using one part only of the folding squab and seat cushion, yet the rear seat which is to be occupied remains perfectly normal and comfortable, even to the folding arm-rest still being in position. The possibilities of this exceedingly clever arrangement seem limitless, and it provides just exactly the variable carrying capacity for which many outdoor motor car users have been yearn-

ing, especially so since the folding portions are strong, straightforward, and perfectly simple. Nevertheless, despite its novelty, this luggage accommodation must not be allowed to overshadow the many other attractive points of the car itself.

The Avon Flying Twenty is a car especially constructed for owners who are looking for specialised coachwork on a well-tried chassis of particular refinement in running, such as the Flying Standard Twenty unquestionably is.

The new Flying Avon Twenty is built as before on this chassis, which has not been altered this year since it is a relatively recent introduction, although based upon components of well-proved reliability. The new Avon saloon is on similar general lines to the 1936 series, but the body is longer and the bonnet slightly shorter. The appearance is greatly improved, for the lines are more flowing and cleaner, especially at the back, where the luggage container swells out from the back panel, and is the full width of the body. The spare wheel is out of sight; it is tucked away horizontally below the floor of the luggage container, and at the front of its compartment is a tool locker of considerable size, in addition to the tool locker under the bonnet in front. The spare wheel locker has its own separate lid, so that luggage need not be disturbed. Apart from the appearance, the new lines have a practical value, for awkward corners and projections are reduced to a minimum, and thus washing and cleaning are rendered easy, particularly so since the wheels are encased by Ace discs.

Within the new coachwork are many features to observe. The steering wheel is mounted telescopically, and the steering column has an instantaneous adjustment to alter the rake, and since the front seat is adjustable, and also the pedals, it is possible for a driver of almost any variety in size to make himself entirely comfortable. All the instruments are grouped clearly in

The new Flying Avon Standard is sporting in appearance, but is a full touring saloon.

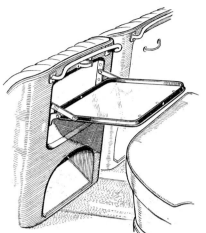

In the rear of the front seats folding tables, hand rails and foot recesses are fitted.

The new model is slightly longer than its predecessor, but the bonnet is shorter.

front of the driver, and in the near side of the scuttle is a large cubby hole.

The front seats are of the bucket type, and are adjustable; in their backs are concealed picnic tables and ash trays, whilst they also carry "grab" handles to assist entry to the rear seats. A "grab" handle is also mounted on the instrument panel, for the near-side forward door. These are unusual fittings in a saloon, but they are none the less distinctly an added convenience.

Arm-rests are mounted on the doors, which have the usual pockets, and there is a folding centre arm-rest to the rear seats, so that three people can be carried at the back if needed. The body is built on best quality ash framing, panelled in sheet steel treated with rust-proof preparation.

At the front the screen pillars are slender along the lines of the driver's vision, so as to eliminate blind spots, and the centre winding windscreen is equipped with twin wiper blades. Centre pillars are eliminated, and the only visible portion between the glasses of the winding windows is a metal slide. Glass anti-draught louvres are provided

over the windows. A flush-fitting sliding roof is fitted, and is devised to avoid causing "storm noise."

Best quality hide is used for the upholstery, and the seats have Dunlopillo overlay. Sun visors are provided, and a refinement in the interior lighting is that there are lights over both rear doors and another over the driving mirror.

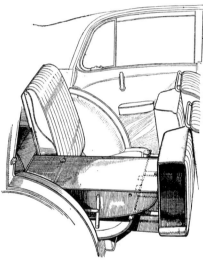

How the folding seat squabs are arranged to form luggage platforms.

One rather striking note in the outer appearance is the adoption of a new form of bonnet louvre, a half-streamline horizontal assembly of chromium slats. These look very well indeed, but are claimed also to have the added virtue of being much more efficient as bonnet ventilators than the orthodox louvre. A wide range of exterior and interior colour schemes is available.

Finally, to give a brief specification of the chassis. The engine is rated at 20 h.p., six cylinders, 73 by 106 mm. (2,663 c.c.). It has side valves, an aluminium high-compression cylinder head, seven-bearing crankshaft, downdraught carburetter with hot-spot induction and air silencer and cleaner. In unit with the engine is a single-plate clutch and four-speed gear box with synchromesh on second, third, and top. The engine and gear box unit has a floating rubber mounting, which secures the elimination of vibration from the car and promotes silence of running.

This chassis is, incidentally, an excellent performer on the road, for it has a sweet and swift acceleration, and an easiness of running over the flats or up the steeper hills which has to be experienced to be appreciated. The refinement of running is marked in every respect. The wheelbase is 9ft. 7¾in., track 4ft. 3½in. The tyres are 5.5 by 17in. Dunlop. D.W.S. permanent four-wheel jacks are fitted. The fuel tank holds twelve gallons.

The Flying Avon Light Twelve drophead coupé, which won many coachwork prizes in rallies during the year, is continued unaltered except in price. This shows a slight increase, being now £255.

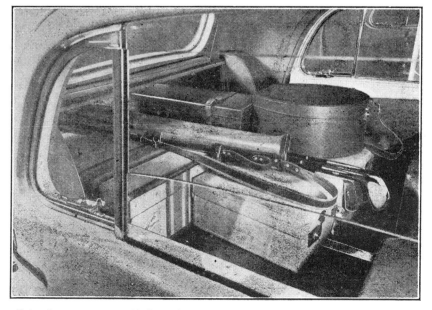

Extra luggage accommodation when the two rear seats are folded as platforms.

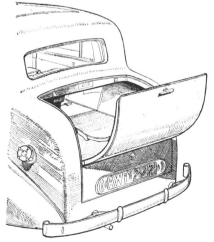

The boot itself is capacious.

More New Cars of 1937

By the HON. MAYNARD GREVILLE

BRITAIN is essentially the home of the small or light car. One of the chief reasons for this is the unique and curious form of taxation which was devised for the motor car in this country. This for many years made it imperative for the British car manufacturer to keep the size of his engine down in order to study the pockets of his customers.

Though the horse-power tax has undoubtedly hampered our manufacturers as far as the export market is concerned, there is also no doubt that at the present time the small car is often more suitable to this island than the large one. Of course for those who go in for continuous long runs the large car has its advantages, but for the ordinary man in this small and crowded island of ours the small car can hold its own.

Even those who own a big car are increasingly coming to realize that the possession of a small car in addition is a distinct advantage and often pays in the long run. It is not always advisable or necessary to take the big car out for short runs, in fact it is generally speaking uneconomic to do so. Many people are finding that a small car used as a sort of tender to the large vehicle saves time and money, not only for those who live in the country, but also for those who have to do their shopping in large towns. It saves getting out the large car every time one wants to run down to the station or the butcher or on some other errand, and prolongs the life and condition of the large car, as short runs with frequent stops are a far greater strain on the mechanism than thousands of miles done continuously on the open road.

In this country we have numerous cars which are excellent for this kind of work. There is, for instance, the Ford Popular model which sells as a two-door saloon for £100, and is only taxed at £6 per annum ; and there is the slightly larger 10 h.p. Ford de luxe at £135.

Morris have several cars which are ideally suited for this class of work. There is the 8 h.p. taxed at £6, which sells at £120 for the saloon and is now a well-tried car that has been on the road for some years. Then there is the larger Ten-Four or Twelve-Four, the first priced at £172 10s., and the latter at £177 10s.

The Hillman Minx is justly famous amongst small cars not only for its handsome appearance but also for its sturdy wearing qualities. This car is taxed at £7 10s., and the price of the saloon is £163.

The Standard Motor Company was one of the first in the field with the light car. A little time ago they brought out a new range of their models starting with the larger cars, which they called Flying Standards. These were distinguished by having a most attractive appearance in addition to a very good performance. Now the range has been extended downwards and starts with the little Flying Standard Nine, which, with its four-cylinder engine, is taxed at £6 15s., and sells as a two-door saloon at £149.

Slightly larger is the Flying Standard Ten, taxed at £7 10s., and selling at £169. Both these models have de luxe forms, for which £10 extra is charged. Amongst the larger cars in this range the Flying Standard Twelve may still be deemed to come within the compass of small cars.

Rover are a firm that made a name for themselves in the very early days of motoring, and have managed to keep up a high standard ever since. In the last few years they have produced a particularly fine range of models, and for 1937 they have not found it necessary to make many changes. The 10-h.p. car is the car in their range which chiefly concerns us here, and for the coming year it is made as a saloon only. It is rated at 10·8 h.p., taxed at £8 5s. and sells for £248.

A handsome and lively small car : the new Flying Standard Nine. (Centre) Captain
J. P. Black, Managing Director of the Standard Motor Co., Ltd.

No. 1,143.—14 h.p.
FLYING STANDARD TOURING SALOON

A Good-looking, Comfortable Car of Medium Size Which Proves Interesting to Drive

COMFORT, roominess of seating, appearance, and performance all have their share in making the Standard Fourteen a decidedly pleasing car, and these qualities are not necessarily set down in order of appeal. This touring saloon tested is an alternative coachwork style to the streamlined Flying saloons, and consists of a smart four-door four-light saloon body provided with a large luggage boot in the tail.

In a manner typical of the current Standard models, the Fourteen possesses a lively and interest-sustaining road performance. It has the acceleration that is so valuable in traffic and on crowded main roads, quite apart from other occasions, and exhibits this about equally from medium as from low speeds, showing up well on top gear. An impression is quickly received of the comparatively big four-cylinder engine giving very satisfactory power in a pleasant way, for it is smooth and quiet to the point of being scarcely noticed at all over the middle range of speed. "Flutter" permitted by the flexible mounting is apparent only if the car is allowed to crawl on top gear, and disappears at about 14 m.p.h., whilst, actually, the engine will pull down to 6 or 7 m.p.h. without setting up transmission snatch.

This car's manner in town traffic is pleasing, it runs particularly nicely through speed-limit areas, and, when the opportunity comes to travel faster on the open road, an effortless engine is observed at speeds that are fast for the great majority of owners. Only when pushed to the very limit does it become really any more noticeable. The speedometer was appreciably optimistic, showing a highest reading of 78, dropping back to 76, and being 4.3 m.p.h. fast at 50, and 2 m.p.h. fast at 30.

From the experiences of a test totalling over 400 miles, mostly done within a two-day period, it can certainly be said that this Standard is able to put up very useful average speeds, comfortably for the passengers and pleasurably to the driver. The latter does not feel tired for any reason connected with the car at the end of a 300-mile run. A long journey in it is in no sense irksome, for there is an air of liveliness and purpose about the whole running, and it is quiet.

In this direction the easy behaviour at speeds between about 50 and 60 m.p.h. counts for much, of course, as, again, does the brisk acceleration, whilst also the general handling is light and responsive. Slopes and lesser main road hills are taken well in the car's stride, and there is an admirable gear change which encourages use of the lower gears on occasion to increase the performance, though in

ordinary driving actual need for dropping down is slight.

Synchromesh is provided on second, third and top and, in conjunction with a comparatively short and rigid lever, placed conveniently, accurate and light gear control is given. The changes go through very nicely. The lower gears are quiet, though not silent. Third will deal with an appreciable gradient, even with three up, and second with a hill of the 1 in 6 type with the same load.

A very satisfactory normal suspension system is found, striking a good compromise between sufficient softness for generally comfortable riding and the firmness needed to secure steady and accurate cornering. Such movement as is produced over less good road surfaces never becomes disturbing, and the car can be taken round bends, and more appreciable corners, too, at speeds a good deal higher than are general practice. It feels safe at speed, sitting down well on the road.

The steering is light, but not by any means very low-geared, rather more than 2¾ turns moving the front wheels from lock to lock. It has good self-centring action, and is not actually heavy at low speed, for a sharp turn or manœuvring, as compared with its pleasing lightness of touch at medium and high speeds. First-rate control is afforded by the brakes, of Bendix type. A soft pressure on the pedal secures all the ordinary decelerations that are wanted, and it is not until more weight is applied that their full inherent power is appreciated. This is very real for braking the car smoothly to a pull-up in an emergency, the wheels remaining on a straight course. They are brakes that allow liberties sometimes to be taken, in the knowledge that the car can be checked just as the driver wants.

A straight-across front seat—at all events as regards the back rest—was fitted. Actually, there are two separate cushions with a recess at the centre in which the hand-brake lever is placed in a convenient position, though the seat

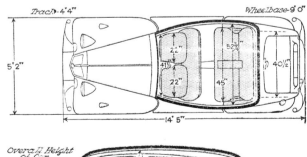

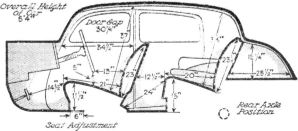

Seating dimensions are measured with cushions and squabs uncompressed

" The Autocar " Road Tests

DATA FOR THE DRIVER

14 h.p. FLYING STANDARD TOURING SALOON.

PRICE, with four-door four-light saloon body, £275. Tax, £10 10s.

RATING : 14 h.p., four cylinders, s.v., 73 × 106 mm., 1,776 c.c.

WEIGHT, without passengers, 25 cwt. 2 qr. 21 lb.

LB. (WEIGHT) PER C.C. : 1.62.

TYRE SIZE : 5.75 × 16in. on bolt-on perforated pressed-steel wheels.

LIGHTING SET : 12-volt ; three-rate charging ; 5 amps. at 30 m.p.h.

TANK CAPACITY : 12 gallons ; approx. normal fuel consumption, 26 m.p.g.

TURNING CIRCLE : (L. and R.) : 37ft. GROUND CLEARANCE : 7in.

ACCELERATION				SPEED	
Overall gear ratios.	From steady m.p.h. of				m.p.h.
	10 to 30	20 to 40	30 to 50	Mean maximum timed speed over ¼ mile	67.16
5.25 to 1	11.0 sec.	12.1 sec.	14.5 sec.	Best timed speed over ¼ mile ...	69.23
7.62 to 1	8.0 sec.	9.5 sec.	14.5 sec.		
12.75 to 1	6.2 sec.	—	—	Speeds attainable on indirect gears (normal and maximum) :—	
20.72 to 1	—	—	—	1st	13—18
From rest to 30 m.p.h. through				2nd	24—31
gears			8.2 sec.	3rd	42—51
To 50 m.p.h. through gears ... 21.2 sec.					
25 yards of 1 in 5 gradient				Speed from rest up 1 in 5 Test	
from rest			5.5 sec.	Hill (on 1st and 2nd gears) ...	16.01

BRAKE TEST : Mean stopping distance from 30 m.p.h., (dry concrete), 30ft.

Performance figures for acceleration and maximum speed are the means of several runs in opposite directions.

(Latest model described in " The Autocar " of July 23rd, 1937.)

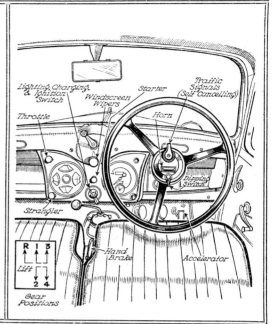

adjustment moves as one. This arrangement always means that driver and front-seat passenger must occupy a similar position irrespective of their heights, but the seat proves comfortable. A slightly more upright squab would be preferred by the driver concerned. Separate front seats are available optionally.

Individual requirements as to driving position are met by the fitting of a telescopically adjustable steering wheel— a valuable feature. One steps straight out in the absence of running boards, and the doors give good openings, but it is not really convenient for the driver to use the near-side door.

At the rear is very considerable space, leg room being increased by a recessed foot-rest let into the base of the front seat. The rear seat cushion places passengers quite low in the car ; at the centre is a wide folding arm-rest. The sliding roof has a one-hand type of central control, the windscreen can be opened out from the centre, there are anti-sunglare visors, and excellent twin-blade screenwipers are fitted. These work from the bottom, go out of sight when not in use, a remote type of electric motor being used, and sweep the whole width of glass. A non-draught venti-lating space is left by reason of the shape of the forward door windows and the provision of glass louvres above, which, incidentally, have some tendency to direct rain water inside the car when a window is opened in wet weather.

The instruments are grouped in two large dials of pleasing appearance, and these, including the trip and total mileage recorders, are well illuminated at night by an attractive non-glare translucent effect. The rear window blind is under the driver's immediate control. A better view could be given by the mirror. The head lamp beam covers the width of the road very well, if not carrying exceptionally far ; the twin-horn note is most adequate and dignified.

A built-in luggage compartment in the tail is of really useful size as to both width and depth, and has a wide external lid which is easily opened or shut, and can also act as a supplementary platform. Laid out in a rubber-lined tray in this lid are the small tools. Below, in a separate compartment with a convenient hinged lid, are the spare wheel and the tools needed for a wheel change, including the portable type of D.W.S. hydraulic jack, for which there is a convenient abutment at each "corner" of the car. A reserve petrol tap is not fitted, but the sensible size of the tank is appreciated on a long journey. An accessible oil filler is provided high up on the engine, and the battery also is under the bonnet. The engine starts at once, and soon gains temperature, as indicated by that interesting and valuable provision—an instrument board thermometer, which is rare on the less expensive cars.

Average-height driver's view through the windscreen of " The Autocar's " Visibility Test scene.

The New Raymond Mays Special

Some Technical Details of a Specialized V8 20 h.p. Model

THE first batch of Raymond Mays chassis, four of which have been entered for the R.A.C. Rally, are now having bodies fitted at the coachbuilders, Messrs. R.E.A.L., of Ealing.

The general specification of these cars is by now well known to enthusiasts, the power unit being based on the V8 Standard, as are certain other chassis components. The engine is rated at 20 h.p. and has a swept volume of 2.6-litres, developing 85 b.h.p. Side valves are employed, these having been specially designed in the light of the

The independent front-wheel suspension layout which embodies transverse leaves and torsion bar.

(Below) Developing: the chassis at the body builders.

high duty requirements of an engine in this type of car.

Cooling is very thorough, there being two water pumps, one for each side of the block, whilst carburation is taken care of by a centrally disposed down-draught instrument.

Deep Frame Members

This power unit with its four-speed synchromesh gearbox, is mounted in a robust frame with a strong X-shaped cross member and underslung at the back. The depth of the frame from the rear portion of the X-member backwards to the rear spring shackle is exceptional and should give great stiffness and good cornering powers.

Controllability is ensured by other features of the design, notably the use of double-acting Armstrong shock absorbers. These are used in conjunction with a neat torsion bar set up, as can be seen from our drawing of the independent front springing, reproduced on this page.

It will be observed that a transverse system is used. This will be interesting on account of the number of leaves employed, a feature which should add

materially to the damping system.

The wheel is also held by a wishbone at the top end and particular care has been taken to give the links of the system a large area so that they will operate for long periods without greasing and without developing play.

The front brakes are 11 ins. diameter and the rear brakes 10 ins.; stiff drums are fitted and the operation system is Bendix-Cowdrey.

The performance of these cars in the R.A.C. Rally, which will be their first public appearance, will be anticipated with interest by all enthusiastic motorists and we hope at an early date to be able to carry out a *Motor* road test, when we expect first-class figures will be obtained.

Three-quarters of a Mile of Wire

CAN you visualize three-quarters of a mile? Try to imagine it as a stretch of road. It is a fair distance to the mind's eye, isn't it? Now see it, not as a road, but as a length of fine wire, and you get an idea of what goes into the secondary winding of a motorcar coil.

To see coil winding machines at work, as one can at the Lucas factory at Birmingham, is to be reminded, curiously, of a cotton mill, for each girl operator sits at a machine which, with its spinning coils and bobbins, is reminiscent of a spinning loom.

The work is skilled, and the operator must be light-fingered, accurate and swift. A long tube is before her as she works, and when her machine is set in motion the shining copper wire can be seen creeping along the tube from right to left, winding the first of 32 layers. A red light glows, the machine stops, the operator varnishes the layer, covers it with paper and starts the motor again, this time from left to right.

Altogether 16,000 turns of the tube are made before the coil winding is complete.

The wire used for the coils is scrupulously tested—and partly by ear. Girls wearing headphones listen while the wire is drawn through a mercury bath, and any fault which may be present is indicated by a warning buzz, while the diameter of the wire is checked on a fluid gauge.

"Autocarrier" Goes Into Service

ON April 3 the Southern Railway motorcar ferryboat "Autocarrier" went into summer service between Dover and Calais. The boat leaves Dover every day at 10.30 a.m. and reaches Calais at noon. The return service leaves at 2.15 p.m. and reaches Dover at 3.45 p.m.

Car freights range from 45s. 6d. upwards according to wheelbase. Single passenger fare is 12s. 6d.

THE NEW FLYING

FOR FINE MOTORING
AT FAR LESS COST!

Petrol consumption 45-48 miles to the gallon . . . Tax only £6 per year . . . Independent front
wheel suspension giving the smoothest possible riding . . . abundant room for four people,
enclosed luggage compartment with lid that opens as a firm, flat platform . . . running that is a
revelation of smooth quietness . . . outstanding top gear pulling and acceleration . . . attractively
streamlined front assembly . . . three-speed synchromesh gears . . . Triplex Glass all round.
That is the New Flying Standard "Eight"! (Open Tourer: Two-four seater body; flush-folding hood;
detachable side-screens; suitcase compartment behind rear seat.)

Saloon £129, Saloon de Luxe £139, Open Tourer £125.

STANDARD "EIGHT"

The AUTOCAR ROAD TESTS

No. 1,282.—8 h.p. FLYING STANDARD DROP-HEAD COUPÉ

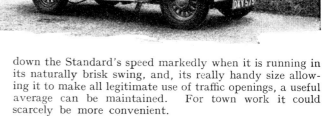

THIS small machine arouses enthusiasm to a quite exceptional extent where the smallest class of car is concerned. The Standard Eight having now been "out" for some eight months, it is perhaps not inappropriate to refer back to remarks made in the first Road Test report on the saloon, in *The Autocar* of September 30th last.

It was then emphasised that the new model showed up so well on the road as to make it seem outstanding among the smallest cars current, and the prediction was offered that it would prove a "winner" in public estimation. The fact that already more than 16,000 Eights have been delivered goes far to support these opinions, which receive further strengthening as the result of the present test of the drop-head coupé.

This model, priced at £159, is the lowest-priced drop-head coupé on the market to-day.

Performance is never everything, and less so probably with small cars than in the case of any other type, but it is little short of phenomenal that a "touring" Eight, as distinct from a sports model, should record a maximum speed by stop-watch exceeding 66 m.p.h. This figure, naturally, was obtained in the favourable direction, and a fair wind was blowing, but the conditions were those uniformly held to in *The Autocar* Tests. The speedometer showed a highest reading of 71, dropping back to about 64 against the wind; at 50 the instrument was 2.8 m.p.h. fast, at 40 2.2, and at 30 1.5 m.p.h.

Similarly, the acceleration tests furnished remarkable figures for a car of this size. In running trim the drop-head coupé is found to be about half a hundredweight lighter than the saloon. The thought arises as to why the Standard should show up so remarkably well, and it might be supposed that the engine is highly stressed. The

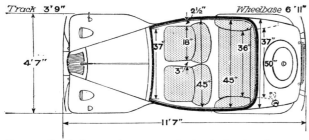

"secret" of the performance obtained lies in the long-stroke design, giving a capacity exceeding one litre and yet retaining an 8 h.p. rating.

At generally used speeds this four-cylinder side-valve engine is smooth and quiet-running, and it has a particularly good ability to pull slowly on top gear. It works smoothly down to even 5 or 6 m.p.h. without transmission snatch, though at that low rate there is gear lever "flutter," this disappearing at about 9 m.p.h. and the car accelerating regularly away on top gear from these low speeds.

It is happily cruised at 50 to 55 m.p.h., and the engine does not become in any way specially noticeable below about a genuine 60 m.p.h. There is naturally increased evidence of the power unit from this rate onwards to the maximum, but a driver who is accustomed to obtaining the most from his car on occasion would not hesitate to employ the available limit in suitable circumstances.

The normal kind of main road gradient does not bring

down the Standard's speed markedly when it is running in its naturally brisk swing, and, its really handy size allowing it to make all legitimate use of traffic openings, a useful average can be maintained. For town work it could scarcely be more convenient.

As to more severe climbing, the usual 1 in 6½ hill was taken very comfortably on second gear from the customary 40 m.p.h. approach, the minimum speed being not below 15 m.p.h., and first gear not being necessary even for the acute corner at the summit. Another illustration of power for climbing is given by the ready way in which this Eight restarted on a genuine 1 in 4 section with a two-up load.

So much for the performance side, wherein a combination of characteristics arising out of able designing leaves the impression of a 10 h.p. rather than an 8 h.p. car.

Independent Front Springing

Another exceptional point among small cars is the possession of independent front wheel suspension, a transverse leaf spring being employed. This suspension has particular merit in taking the shocks out of even a potholed surface, and is sufficiently firm for cornering purposes, the car not tending to heel over unless specially fast tactics are adopted. Actual fore-and-aft pitching is avoided, though over some kinds of surfaces at medium and fairly fast speeds there is a certain amount of bouncing motion.

The steering is finger-light but high geared, needing only 2⅓ turns of the wheel from lock to lock, and is accurate enough at all speeds to make the driver confident. It has some caster action and does not transmit road wheel shocks. This is a very easy car to manœuvre and turn about. The brakes are cable-operated Bendix, and give

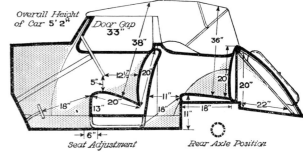

Seating dimensions are measured with cushions and squabs uncompressed.

" The Autocar " Road Tests

DATA FOR THE DRIVER   26-5-39

8 H.P. FLYING STANDARD DROP-HEAD COUPÉ.

PRICE, with two-door drop-head coupé body, £159. Tax £6.

RATING : 8.06 h.p., four cylinders, s.v., 57 × 100 mm., 1,021 c.c.

WEIGHT, without passengers, 14 cwt. 2 qr. 17 lb. LB. PER C.C. : 1.61.

TYRE SIZE : 4.75 × 16in. on bolt-on perforated pressed-steel wheels.

LIGHTING SET : 6-volt. Automatic voltage control.

TANK CAPACITY : 6 gallons ; approx. normal fuel consumption 36—46 m.p.g.

TURNING CIRCLE : (L. and R.) : 34ft.   GROUND CLEARANCE : 7in.

ACCELERATION				SPEED.	
Overall gear ratios	From steady m.p.h. of			Mean maximum timed speed	m.p.h.
	10 to 30	20 to 40	30 to 50	over ¼ mile	62.07
5.14 to 1	13.9 sec.	15.5 sec.	19.5 sec.	Best timed speed over ¼ mile ...	66.18
8.63 to 1	8.1 sec.	10.3 sec.	—	Speeds attainable on indirect	
18.75 to 1	—	—	—	gears (normal and maximum) :—	
From rest to 30 m.p.h. through				1st	14—20
gears			8.7 sec.	2nd	33—45
To 50 m.p.h. through gears			25.3 sec.		
25 yards of 1 in 5 gradient				Speed from rest up 1 in 5 Test	
from rest			—*	Hill	—*

* Brooklands Test Hill not fully available.

BRAKE TEST : Mean stopping distance from 30 m.p.h. (damp concrete), 33.5ft.

WEATHER : Showers, mild ; wind fresh, S.W. Barometer : 29.30in.

Performance figures for acceleration and maximum speed are the means of several runs in opposite directions, with two up.

(Chassis described in " The Autocar " of September 30th, 1938.)

---

capital retarding power with a light pedal pressure.

Synchromesh is provided on top and second of the three-speed gear box, thus acting on both upward changes. Fairly quick changes can be made, if required, without clashing, though the engagement is sometimes a little " sticky." To engage first gear at appreciable road speed calls for double-declutching, but except for starting purposes, as has been made clear, in average country this ratio is not likely to be wanted much. It is fairly audible, but second gear is quieter. The lever is firm and of convenient length.

A comfortable driving position is obtained. The thin-rimmed steering wheel is mounted a trifle high to some people's way of thinking, but on the whole conveniently arranged. The separate seats give a fairly upright position with plenty of support ; the passenger seat is not provided with an adjustment. A pull-and-push type of hand-brake lever is within fairly convenient reach, and holds securely on a 1 in 4 gradient. It is not easy for the driver to use the near-side door.

The instruments are neatly grouped and have clearly marked faces, well illuminated at night by a translucent system. They do not include a clock, and the speedometer has no trip mileage recorder. The windscreen can be opened by means of a central winding control. Beneath the instrument board is a very useful shelf. The driving mirror is mounted externally ; it was hardly visible to a driver sitting fairly well forward, but a longer bracket is now fitted. The horn note is not particularly strong, but is adequate. The head lamps give a sufficient beam, though not of specially long range.

Although the rear seats are to be regarded in the nature of occasional accommodation, and are somewhat " blind " from the point of view of the occupants, very fair two-seater accommodation of an extra nature is afforded by them.

There is an interior luggage compartment, reached by hinging forward the back seat squab, to the inside of which are attached the wheel-changing and other big tools. The drop-head is freed by unclipping two quick-action fasteners. It is easily lowered and goes down flat, affording a clear view behind and giving a very good open car effect, the winding windows in the doors being available for protection. The head is easily raised again and secured to the windscreen frame. There is some slight tendency for the fabric to flap at fairly high speed in a wind.

A normal centrally hinged bonnet is used, good access being given to the engine for general inspection and attention. It starts at once and pulls away well from cold without much use of the mixture control.

Dotted lines show the windscreen frame as seen with the head open. The screen is shallow but quite wide ; its pillars are thick.
Excellent vision is afforded over the bonnet, though neither wing is seen by an average-height driver sitting fairly close.

THEY'RE NEW—THEY'RE NEWS!

THE NEW FLYING STANDARD "TEN" SUPER SALOON (£185)

Petrol consumption 38-40 miles per gallon! Roomy enclosed luggage boot . . . Independent front wheel suspension . . . Top gear speed over 63 m.p.h. Flush-fitting sliding roof, 12-volt electrical equipment, 4-speed synchromesh gearbox. New design four-door all-steel body giving maximum body space. Front seats independently adjustable. **Other 10 h.p. models :** **Saloon £169, Saloon de Luxe, with attractive additional equipment, £179.**

THE NEW FLYING STANDARD " TWELVE " DE LUXE (£225)

Petrol consumption 30-32 miles per gallon. Four five-seater body—with folding centre rear arm-rest, opening quarter lights, window louvres, and a lavish list of refinements. Roomy enclosed luggage boot with lid that opens as a firm, flat platform for trunks. Telescopic steering column, independent front wheel suspension, automatic chassis lubrication, 12-volt electrical equipment. 70 m.p.h. **£225 ex works. Other 12 h.p. models :** **Saloon £205, Drop-Head Coupé £245.**

TWO OTHER ATTRACTIVE MODELS

THE FLYING STANDARD "NINE" SUPER SALOON (£165)

Another splendidly thrifty model! Capable of 40 miles per gallon! Taxed at only £6. 15. 0! Maximum speed is a steady 62 m.p.h. Features include enclosed luggage boot, (lid forms flat luggage platform) 4-speed synchromesh gears, 12-volt electrical equipment, flush-fitting sliding roof, Triplex Glass all round and roomy four-seater all-steel body. **Other 9 h.p. models: Saloon £149, Saloon de luxe, with attractive additional equipment, £159.**

THE FLYING STANDARD "TOURING SALOONS"— "FOURTEEN" (£268) AND "TWENTY" (£325)

The successful "Touring Saloons" in 1939 form — with attractive new improvements including imposing chromium-finished radiator, wind-horns with dual tone switch, fog lamp, and luxurious unpleated upholstery. They are cars of most exceptional convenience and distinction—*and especially noteworthy for their unusually roomy seating and generous luggage accommodation.* The full five-seater saloons have exceptional head, leg and elbow room, six side windows and a large rear window, their equipment includes side arm-rests, folding centre arm-rest, folding tables, opening quarter-lights and louvres to each door window. There is a large enclosed luggage boot, giving accommodation for several suitcases or four golf bags. Its lid opens to form a firm, flat, additional luggage platform for trunks. **Other 14 h.p. models: Saloon (£249) and Drop-head Coupé (£288).**

An Entirely New Model!

- **INDEPENDENT FRONT WHEEL SUSPENSION.**
- **FOUR-DOOR FOUR-SEATER ALL-STEEL BODY WITH AMPLE LUGGAGE ACCOMMODATION.**
- **BUILT FOR ECONOMY—**
- **LOW TAX.** 45-48 M.P.G.

The near side front wheel, showing the INDEPENDENT SPRINGING Assembly

The large Luggage Boot has ample room for several Suitcases.
The lid opens to form a strong flat luggage platform.

CHASSIS ...

ENGINE. 4 Cylinders. 57 m.m. × 100 m.m. s... R.A.C. rating 8.06. Improved "Buoyant Powe... valves. Three bearing counter-balanced cranksha... Harmonic cams. Aluminium pistons. Thermo... aluminium cylinder head. High efficiency comb... block. Hot spot induction pipe. Down draug... lubrication, floating oil intake. Flexibly mounte... advance. Air-cooled dynamo. Compensated vo...

TRANSMISSION. Three-speed gearbox, central... gears. Accessible gearbox filler with dip-stick. ... universal joints with needle roller bearings. Si... 2nd, 8.87 ; 1st, 19.29 ; reverse, 23.72.

REAR AXLE. Semi-floating with pressed steel...

FRAME AND SPRINGS. Chassis frame, box se... wells. Welded joints. Independent front wheel... $36\frac{1}{4}'' \times 2\frac{1}{4}''$; semi-elliptic rear springs, $39'' \times 1\frac{1}{2}''$... Luvax piston type hydraulic shock absorbers fro... side-lift jacking system. "Easy-clean" pressed s...

BRAKES. Bendix duo-servo. Operation by ha... Steel brake drums, $1\frac{1}{4}'' \times 8''$ front, $1\frac{1}{2}'' \times 6''$ rear. ...

STEERING. Burman-Douglas worm and nut. ... diameter.

ELECTRICAL SYSTEM. 6-volt. Lucas batter...

PERFORMANCE.		CO...
BRAKE HORSE POWER.		
R.P.M.	H.P.	At 30 m.p...
1,000	8	
2,000	18	At 40 m.p...
3,000	27	At 50 m.p...
4,250 (Peak)	33	
MAXIMUM SPEEDS.		Average o...
Top gear	60 m.p.h.	
2nd gear	40 m.p.h.	Oil ..

SALOON

BODY DETAILS

BODY. Four-door, six-light, four-seater saloon. All-steel construction. Finished synthetic enamel. Wings and wheels the same colour as body. Front wing splash guards. Flush-fitting sliding roof.

UPHOLSTERY. Fine quality leather cloth (Saloon). Fine furniture hide (Saloon de luxe).

SEATING. Front seats of bucket type. Driver's seat adjustable. Wide rear seat (37 inches effective) ; no footwells.

EQUIPMENT. Self-cancelling illuminated direction indicators ; foot-operated headlamp dip-switch, anti-dazzle system ; Triplex safety glass to all windows and screen ; electric screen wiper, motor mounted in scuttle ; translucent illuminated instrument panel with large dials (incorporating ammeter, electric petrol gauge, oil pressure gauge, speedometer) ; ignition lock ; stop light ; chromium-plated bumper bars ; locks to doors ; inside driving mirror ; concealed rear window blind, driver operated ; electric horn ; door windows fitted with winders ; sun visor ; adjustable front seats ; hair carpets with underfelt ; full tool kit.

THE FOUR-DOOR SALOON DE LUXE has the following extra equipment : Fine furniture hide upholstery ; opening windscreen ; chromium plated lamps ; roof light ; ash trays.

LUGGAGE. Ample accommodation for suitcases in boot, lid of which opens as a strong, flat luggage platform. Spare wheel and tyre in separate enclosed compartment beneath locker. Parcel accommodation in a tray below instrument panel.

COLOUR SCHEMES.

BODY COLOUR	..	..	..	Black	Blue	Grey
TRIMMING	..	..	..	Brown	Blue	Blue

LS

acity 1021 c.c. Comp. ratio 6.7. engine mounting. Side by side nnecting rods, precision bearings. d fan cooling system. Die-cast mbers. Chromium iron cylinder er. Air silencer. Pressure type ystem. Coil ignition, automatic l of dynamo charge rate.

Synchro-mesh and silent helical er all-metal propeller shaft and e clutch. Top gear ratio, 5.29 ;

piral bevel final drive.

d steel, low level to avoid foot-, transverse semi-elliptic spring. ntbloc'' bushes ; controlled by . Easily operated and accessible

o all wheels by enclosed cables. ndbrake under scuttle.

le 35 feet. Steering wheel, 16½"

apacity.

	TOP GEAR ACCELERATION (Two up).		DIMENSIONS.		INTERIOR DIMENSIONS.	
52 m.p.g.	10 to 30 m.p.h. .. 14 secs.	Tyre Size .. .. .. 4.75—16		Width of rear seat, effective	37″
45 m.p.g.	30 to 50 m.p.h. .. 20 secs.	Wheelbase .. .. .. 7′ 4″		Maximum interior width ..	48″
	0 to 50 through the	Track .. .. .. 3′ 9″		Width of front seats, each ..	19½″
36 m.p.g.	gears .. .. 28 secs.	Ground clearance (under axle) 7″			
		Length (luggage locker closed) 12′ 0″		Height from floor to roof,	
45 m.p.g.	**BRAKES**	Width .. .. .. 4′ 7″		maximum	49″
	SPEED STOPPING DISTANCE	Height (unladen) .. .. 5′ 2″		Depth of rear seat	18″
00 m.p.g.	From 30 m.p.h. .. 30 feet	Weight (no petrol) .. 15½ cwt.		Depth of front seat	18″
	From 40 m.p.h. .. 60 feet	Petrol tank capacity .. 6 gallons			

A LIST OF PRE-WAR STANDARD CARS

1903: **6hp**
1904: **Three-cylinder**
1904: **12/15hp**
1905: **16hp**
1905-08: **18/20hp**
1906: **10hp**
1906: **24/30hp**
1906-12: **50hp**
1906: **Bradburn Car**
1906: **The Lindsey**
1907: **15hp**
1907: **30hp**
1908-11: **20hp**
1908-11: **40hp**
1909-11: **16hp**
1910-11: **12hp Model J**
1911-12: **20hp**
1912: **15hp Model K**
1912: **25hp**
1913-14: **20hp**
1913-15: **Model S "Rhyl"**
1918: **Model S "Rhyl"**
1919-21: **Model SLS**
1921-23: **Model SLO**
1921-23: **8hp**
1922-26: **Model SLO-4**
1924-27: **Model V3**
1926-28: **Model V4**
1926-28: **Model 6V 18/36**
1927-29: **9hp**
1928: **Model 6V 18/42**

1928-30: **9hp LWB**
1929-31: **15hp SWB**
1929-33: **16hp LWB**
1930-33: **Big Nine**
1930-35: **Envoy**
1931-35: **Twenty**
1932-33: **Little Nine**
1932-33: **Little Twelve**
1932-33: **Big Twelve**
1934: **Twelve-Six**
1934-36: **Nine**
1934-36: **Ten**
1934-36: **10/12 Speed Model**
1934-36: **Twelve**
1934-36: **Sixteen**
1935-36: **Twenty**
1935-36: **Flying Twelve**
1935-36: **Flying Sixteen**
1935-39: **Flying Twenty**
1936: **Flying Ten**
1936 : **Light Twelve**
1936: **Flying Light Twelve**
1936: **Light Twenty**
1936-38: **V8**
1937-40: **Flying Nine**
1937-40: **Flying Ten**
1937-40: **Flying Light Twelve**
1937-40: **Flying Fourteen 12**
1937-40: **Flying Fourteen 14**
1937-40: **Flying Twenty**
1938-40: **Flying Eight**

THE STANDARD MOTOR CLUB

The Standard Motor Club is a worldwide organisation, run by an elected committee in accordance with the RAC guidelines. It's aims are to promote interest in, use and the preservation of all Standard and Standard-based vehicles. It is the only owner's club that caters for the full range of Standard cars. The Club provides a professionally-produced forty page magazine ten times a year, technical advice, help with spares, a library facility and numerous social events throughout the year. Membership details can be obtained from:

Tony Pingriff,
Membership Secretary,
Standard Motor Club,
57 Main Road,
Meriden,
Coventry,
CV7 7LP.